Elegant Wire Jewelry

Elegant Wire Jewelry

Contemporary Designs
&
Creative Techniques

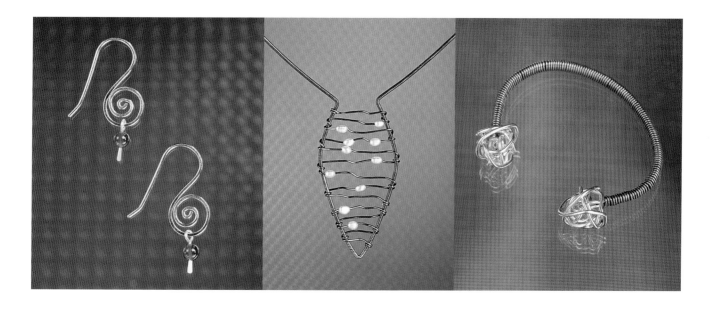

Kathy Frey

LARK BOOKS

A Division of Sterling Publishing Co., Inc.
New York

DEVELOPMENT EDITOR: Terry Taylor

EDITOR: Jean Campbell

ART DIRECTOR: Kathleen Holmes

COVER DESIGNER: Cindy LaBreacht

ASSISTANT EDITOR: Nathalie Mornu

ASSOCIATE ART DIRECTOR: Shannon Yokeley

ART PRODUCTION ASSISTANT: Jeff Hamilton

EDITORIAL ASSISTANCE: Delores Gosnell

PHOTOGRAPHERS:

PROJECT PHOTOGRAPHY:
Stewart O'Shields

HOW-TO PHOTOGRAPHY:
Blackbox Photography (Steve Mann)

Library of Congress Cataloging-in-Publication Data

Frey, Kathleen Ann, 1972-
    Elegant wire jewelry : contemporary designs & creative techniques /
Kathleen Ann Frey. — 1st ed.
        p.   cm.
    Includes index.
    ISBN 1-57990-908-6 (hardcover)
    1. Jewelry making.   2. Wire craft.   I. Title.
TT212.F74 2007
745.594'2—dc22

                                        2006034667

10 9 8 7 6 5 4 3 2

First Edition

Published by Lark Books, A Division of Sterling Publishing Co., Inc.
387 Park Avenue South, New York, N.Y. 10016

Distributed in Canada by Sterling Publishing, c/o Canadian Manda Group,
165 Dufferin Street, Toronto, Ontario, Canada M6K 3H6

Distributed in the United Kingdom by GMC Distribution Services, Castle Place,
166 High Street, Lewes, East Sussex, England BN7 1XU

Distributed in Australia by Capricorn Link (Australia) Pty Ltd., P.O. Box 704,
Windsor, NSW 2756 Australia

If you have questions or comments about this book, please contact:
Lark Books
67 Broadway
Asheville, NC 28801
(828) 253-0467

Manufactured in China

ISBN 13: 978-1-57990-908-6

ISBN 10: 1-57990-908-6

For information about custom editions, special sales, premium and corporate
purchases, please contact Sterling Special Sales Department at 800-805-5489 or
specialsales@sterlingpub.com.

Contents

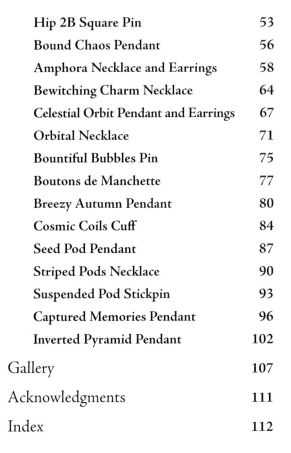

Introduction

The thing I love most about wire is its potential. Here's a raw material, used to make notebook binding, hangers, fences, and cable, that when taken out of its utilitarian context and manipulated a bit differently, can become something unexpectedly beautiful.

I remember my first experiences working with wire to make jewelry. When I was a teenager, I made a lot of beaded jewelry, so wire was always an option as a stringing material, along with threads and cords. After college, I worked in a bead store, just when making wire jewelry with a jig was starting to hit the crafting world. I tried my hand at this wireworking technique but still relied heavily on beads to make beautiful and interesting designs.

Then one day it hit me: Wire itself could be the main focus of my jewelry! When I think about that time in my life—that "ah ha" moment—my heart still races with excitement. I realized then and there that using a wire jig was fun but limiting, and that I wanted to make pieces and shapes that were my own inventions. My mind was flooded with questions: Do wire shapes always have to be flat or can they be dimensional? What types of wire are available? Can I change the color of wire? The questions kept running through my mind, and suddenly there weren't enough hours in a day to explore the possibilities. Luckily for you, some of the answers I found are right here in this book and will help jump-start you into making your own wire jewelry.

I find that one of the best aspects of making wire jewelry is that it's rewarding; you can finish a piece very quickly without needing a lot of specialty tools. And that kind of near-instant gratification is easy to achieve once you have some basic techniques under your belt. You'll build a good foundation by trying some of the projects in the beginning of this book; then you can develop as you try more complex projects. For instance, if you have your own bead collection or just enjoy color, start off with the Dancing Branches Necklace and Earring set on page 48. Only three tools from the Basic Tool Kit are required for the basic necklace construction in this project (chain-nose pliers, round-nose pliers, and wire cutters), and the project employs the simple loop (see Basics, page 18). It will also introduce you to making your own clasps—a great technique to know for any type of jewelry making.

If you want to learn slightly more complex wire-manipulation techniques, try the Bewitching Charm Necklace on page 64. It will help you get comfortable with bending wire into shapes. Then use what you've learned to make the Amphora Necklace on page 58, which will introduce you to simple wire wrapping. Both projects use hammering techniques, and if you make the matching earrings, you can try your hand at filing as well.

As you become comfortable working with wire, you can take more time and experiment with the different ways to finish your wirework with patinas and textures. If you're really enjoying yourself, try more complex wrapped forms like the Inverted Pyramid Pendant on page 102, or use what you've learned to make forms of your own design. These take more practice and patience, but the instructions are provided in steps, so you can set a piece aside and come back to it later if you wish. Or, if you're like me, you'll become a little obsessed and will want to finish a piece just to see how it turns out. One of my greatest pleasures is to see how each piece looks a little different when it's finished, just because each one is handmade.

Once you've tried some or all of the projects, I predict you too will have questions about the possibilities of wireworking running through your mind. Those questions will fuel your creativity and help you come up with designs and ideas of your own. Don't be afraid to experiment or try something new. After all, it's only wire—the stuff of champagne cork cages and twist ties. It's a humble medium that we can make great by tapping into its limitless potential.

top: **Kathy Frey**, *Black Gold Cluster Neckring*, 2005
Oxidized sterling silver, 14K gold
Photo by Larry Sanders

bottom: **Kathy Frey**, *Ring Collection*, 2006
Mixed media including sterling silver, 14K gold, 18K gold, carnelian, rubber
Photo by Larry Sanders

The Basics

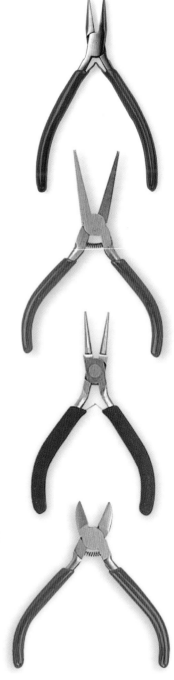

tools

The only tools that are absolutely necessary for making jewelry with wire are chain-nose pliers, round-nose pliers, and a pair of wire cutters. I worked for years with only these three basic tools. Over time, though, I've learned more techniques and expanded my basic repertoire of skills to include some other fun and simple designs, as well as more refined finishing techniques.

For the purposes of the projects in this book, I've described two tool kits: A Basic Tool Kit and a Beyond-the-Basics Tool Kit so you'll know what to have on hand. To try out most of the techniques explained in the projects, pick up the tools in the first kit. Purchase the tools in the Beyond-the-Basics Kit if you want to make each and every one of the projects. And, if you find yourself fully committed to making wire jewelry, give in and get the tools for a Fully Committed Tool Junkie, too.

What you won't find in these lists are the things you're likely have on hand: a fine-point permanent marker, simple forms around which to wrap wire, such as round pens, pencils, dowels, or cans; tape; paper; and string.

Basic Tool Kit

Chain-nose pliers are flat and smooth on the inside so they don't mar the wire when grasping it. The jaws taper to a fine point for detailed manipulation. These pliers are used for all wire handling and grasping, as well as for bending.

Flat-nose pliers have flat, wide jaws and are used primarily for grasping and bending wire.

Round-nose pliers have jaws that look like tapered cones. These pliers are used exclusively for making loops or rounded shapes. They should not be used to grasp the wire, as they put pressure on it and can weaken it by forming an indent.

Jeweler's wire cutters have very sharp blades that come to a fine point. When cutting a piece of wire, the blades will leave one side with a V-cut and the other side with a flat (or *flush*) cut.

Tip

Buy all of your pliers at a bead or craft store rather than a hardware store so they are the appropriately sized for making jewelry. Comfort is important to reduce wear and tear on your hands, so explore different types of pliers and cutters to see which are most comfortable for you. For example, some have ergonomic handles and/or springs, while others don't. As you shop, you'll notice that more expensive pliers and cutters have finer points and tend to feel more solid in your grasp.

Wet/dry sandpaper is used for final hand finishing. It's available at hardware stores in a wide range of grits. The best grits for wirework are 320-, 400-, and 600-grit.

Abrasive scouring pads are used to achieve matte finishes. You can buy these pads at hardware and grocery stores.

A **flat metal ruler** is necessary for measuring wire and other materials. Use one that's at least a 12 inches (30.5 cm) long and that is also marked for metric measurements.

Safety glasses protect your eyes, especially when you're cutting wire or working with the long wires that you'll use for wrapping; these can whip around and catch you off guard.

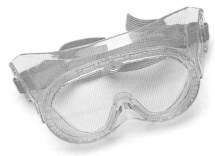

Basic flat files can be found at your local hardware store. For wirework, the file doesn't need to be any longer than 7 inches (17.8 cm). This type of file is used mostly for shaping pin stems or on forms from which a lot of metal must be removed.

Needle files come in sets that include a variety of shapes. My favorite is a barette file, which is flat, pointed, and tapered on one side to get into tight spots, and which has a smooth, peaked back side so you don't accidentally cut into a wire that's nearby. When buying files, the smaller the better; a length of 4 to 6 inches (10.2 to 15.2 cm) is best.

Beyond-the-Basics Tool Kit

A **steel block** is the surface upon which you'll do any hammering or burnishing. A small 2½ x 2½-inch (6.4 x 6.4 cm) block is fine, but if you think you'll love making jewelry with wire, go ahead and purchase a 6 x 6-inch (15.2 x 15.2 cm) block. The larger block gives you more options for working with longer pieces of wire (for example, when you're making stick pins).

A **small planishing hammer**, unlike jewelers' hammers designed to hit other tools, is used to hammer your final product. The head is very fine, flat, smooth, and hard. I prefer a small riveting hammer because my pieces are small and I don't do heavy forming. The small head allows for fine control, so there are fewer marks left behind.

A **burnisher** is a common stone-setting tool that features a long, gently curved tip. It's great for hardening and straightening small pieces of wire.

Liver of sulfur and other oxidizing solutions give wire a darkened appearance. Follow the manufacturer's instructions when using these products, as they can sometimes be toxic.

Metal brushes shine the wire after it's been oxidized and can also be used to texturize finished pieces.

The Fully-Committed-Tool-Junkie Kit

Texturizing hammers are used to make textured patterns in the wire. They include ball peen, cross peen, and chasing hammers, each of which leaves its own unique mark.

Specialty pliers do very specific tasks, such as making jump rings, straightening wire, and grasping wire in very tight places.

Mandrels are specifically shaped, solid metal forms that help uniformly shape and size jewelry pieces. They come in different types, including oval and round bracelet and ring versions. In a pinch you can use wooden dowels, metal tubing, and even knitting needles as mandrels.

wire

You'll need only one material—wire—to make every project in this book. Wire can be made out of any type of metal and comes in a variety of profiles, only one of which is round! When I was just getting started, I bought wire at the hardware store. Most hardware stores have a section of copper, steel, and iron wire on small spools. These base-metal wires are a great and inexpensive material to use. Other inexpensive options available from craft, hobby, and bead stores include nickel silver and brass wires. Until you become comfortable working with wire, practice or experiment with an inexpensive kind.

If you love color, look for color-coated copper wires, which are available at many craft, hobby, and bead stores. These are less expensive and softer to work with than niobium—another colored wire that is available through many jewelry suppliers and online sources. Color-coated copper wire is as easy to work with as copper. Take care that you don't nick or mar the surface with your tools. Otherwise, you can hammer and manipulate it.

You can also find wire in places other than hardware or craft stores. When you keep your eyes open to the possibilities, you'll find some other fun options to play with, such as aluminum armature wire, plastic-coated telephone wire, electrical wire, and steel cable.

If the look of copper, brass, or colored wire doesn't appeal to you, use precious metal wires. Don't be tempted by inexpensive silver- or gold-plated wires; the plating is easy to scratch and will often pop off during manipulation. The most affordable options are sterling silver, fine silver, and gold-filled wires. Fine silver is appealing because it doesn't tarnish, but it's also extremely soft, which makes it difficult to manipulate. Sterling silver is stronger, harder, and easier to bend. Gold-filled wire is high-quality wire with an actual layer of karat gold that's been heat- and pressure-bonded to a brass surface, which makes it extremely durable and an affordable option if you have metal allergies. If you wish to splurge, all types and colors of wire are available in solid gold in various karats, as well as in platinum and other types of precious metals.

Most precious metal wires are also available in shapes other than round. Square, triangular, half-round, domed, rectangular, twisted, and patterned wire can all be purchased. I create all of my designs with round wire, and all of the projects in this book use round wire, but feel free to try working with square, half-round, or other wire shapes—you'll be amazed at how different they can make a design look.

Wire Properties

Each type of wire has its own properties, such as thickness, hardness, and malleability, as well as surface color and reactivity (in other words, whether it will tarnish or can receive a patina). The properties of the wire you purchase will affect how easy or difficult it is use and how the finished piece will look.

Gauge

Wire comes in different gauges (or thicknesses): the higher the number, the smaller the diameter. In general, you can purchase threadlike wires as small as 36-gauge, up to gauges 1 or 2, which look more like metal rods than wire.

Since I do a lot of my work by hand, I generally don't work with anything heavier than 16-gauge wire, and anything smaller than 28-gauge feels too delicate. I usually don't go smaller than 26-gauge for my designs.

For most of the projects in this book, we'll use 18-, 20-, 22-, 24-, and 26-gauge wire, in both soft and half-hard options.

Hardness

Some wires are naturally harder or softer than others, and thicker gauge wires are naturally harder than thinner ones. I learned a lot about hardness by trying different designs with different types of wire, sometimes successfully and sometimes not. After you purchase wire, you can make it harder or softer (see the techniques described on page 15). Since I work with a lot of wire, I often buy mine prehardened—it's easier and saves me a lot of time. The most common hardness options for sterling silver, gold-filled, and other high-end wires are dead soft, half-hard, and hard.

You can also harden copper, brass, and nickel silver yourself, but you can only buy it in its soft state. Fine silver is only available as soft and doesn't harden much, so it's generally too soft and delicate to use for these projects, which is unfortunate because it doesn't tarnish. There's also a new type of sterling silver available on the market called *argentium*. It acts just like sterling silver but is slower to tarnish and is becoming more commonly available in all gauges and findings.

Manipulating Wire

The most important thing I've found over my years of wirework is to avoid repetitive stress. Different wireworking activities (wrapping, hammering, and making balls) place stress on your hands, arms, and shoulders in different ways, so take a break every once in a while and vary the types of projects you do. You can exercise your hands by squeezing a tennis ball, and stretch your hands and wrists by gently bending back the fingers on each hand, while extending your arm. It's also important to stretch your neck and shoulders, since the tendency is to hunch over this kind of detailed work.

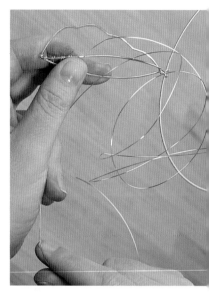

Your hands and fingers will still get tired no matter what you do, so you may want to use adhesive bandages on your fingers to help you hold the wire.

Working with wire, especially with long wrapping lengths, takes patience. Wire has a lot of body and often seems to have a mind of its own. If you get into wire as a medium, though, you will learn how to gauge your mood. When I'm feeling short-tempered or overcaffeinated, I work with shorter wire pieces and usually incorporate some hammering. When I'm mellow and listening to a good audiobook or album, I tackle a large wrapping project and find it soothing to work with the long pieces.

Tips

Don't put on hand lotion right before starting a wireworking project because the wire will slide right through your fingers and you won't be able to get a grip on it.

In general, I like to start my projects with a little more wire than is called for. Wire gets hard to manipulate in short lengths, so adding a little extra at the get-go means much less frustration later. All of the projects in this book have a little extra wire built into their measurements, but feel free to work with lengths that are comfortable for you. I think the easiest lengths to work with are between 6 inches (15.2 cm) and 2 feet (61 cm). When working with wire that's shorter than 6 inches (15.2 cm), you'll need to rely on your pliers more in order to manipulate it. And when you're working with wire longer than 2 feet (61 cm), you'll need to watch where it goes—make sure you're wearing eye protection because the wire definitely twists and flies around.

Cutting Wire

There are many different types of wire cutters available. I've tried several different kinds, and I must confess that I love my 11-year old pair, which I bought for almost nothing at a bead store. Whatever types you use, purchase them from a craft or bead store—not from your local hardware store—so they are the appropriate size for the scale of the work.

Whenever you're cutting wire, make sure to point your cutters down. If possible, hold both pieces of wire to prevent either end from flying out of control. Some pliers come with wire retainers that prevent the wire from flying. Most basic wire cutters cut in a similar manner: when you cut a piece of wire, one cut end will be *flush cut* and the other will be pointed. All of my projects refer to flush cutting—the process of cutting a wire so its end is flat (or flush).

Finishing Cut Ends

After you've finished a coil or wrap and trimmed the wire, sometimes the wire end will only need to be flush cut and squeezed with pliers so that it pops into alignment. With heavier wires or when you can feel the cut end of the wire sticking out, you

will need to tuck in (or flatten) the tail slightly by giving it a squeeze as you rotate the pliers in the direction of the coil.

Filing and Sanding

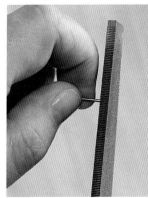

If a wire end is purposely exposed and needs to be finished smooth, the first step is to file it with a flat file. For a flat, squared-off end, work with a flat file and file the end in one direction until there is no resistance and the cut end has a smooth reflection in the light. If possible, work with a file that's wider

than the cut surface; a wide file will make it easier to achieve a level end.

To file an end to a point for a pin stem, work with a larger flat file. Hold the file at a 45°angle to the wire and file in an upward direction (from base to point), while rotating the wire until a sharp point is formed.

If you want the point to be extra sharp, block out the cone-shaped point with a large file as described, then refine it with a smaller needle file before proceeding to sanding.

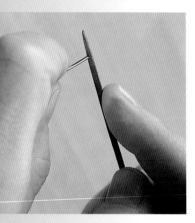

To form a rounded end on the wire, as for an ear wire, curve the file over the tip of the wire to prevent a point from being formed. Make smaller motions than you would to make a sharp point; you don't want a longer cone shape. I often do this with a flat needle file because it's easier for me to manipulate than a large flat file.

Sometimes you have to file the wire in a specific way—one that corresponds to the jewelry's shape. For example, some wire frame projects in this book end with a coil that requires a partially rounded edge that is smooth to the touch. For this type of filing, I use

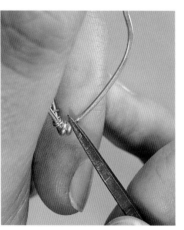

needle-nose files, and file in one direction, curving the file on the wire to get the shape that's needed.

Any exposed, cut area that's been filed must be sanded smooth. Use three basic grades of sandpaper available at any hardware store: 320-, 400-, and 600-grit.

Start with 320-grit sandpaper. Sand in one direction and pay attention to any wire edges that might have sharp

bumps (or *burrs*) left over from the filing. Tear off small pieces of the paper and manipulate them to do what you need them to do. The main purpose of using 320-grit sandpaper first is to remove burrs and start smoothing the surface; it doesn't take long.

Repeat the process with the 400-grit sandpaper (I spend the most time with this grit) and then finish with the 600-grit paper. When you are finished, the piece should be totally smooth to the touch.

Straightening Wire

When you buy wire, it will be on some sort of spool or in a coil, so when you cut a piece to work with, the piece will have a natural curve. Some projects work with this natural curve, and most wrapping works with this curve, as well. When you're wrapping a long piece of wire, wrap with the curve instead of against it, so the wire curves into your piece. You can keep the wire from kinking by gently pulling and curving it between your fingers to maintain the gentle natural curve. Do this anytime you see the wire starting to bend on itself or twisting to form a kink.

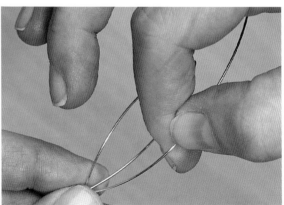

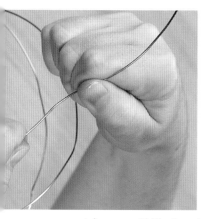

Of course there are times when you don't want the curve in the wire. A significant amount of straightening can be done with your fingers. Simply pull the wire between your thumb and forefinger, applying pressure against the curve of the wire. Use only a small amount of pressure and repeat until the wire is as straight as you'd like it to be. Most of my work is freeform, so I like this casual technique.

When you're wrapping a geometric form, you want to wrap with the curve of the wire, but ultimately you want the individual wraps to be straight. To achieve this end, keep the wire curved until you're ready to secure the wrap. Then pull the desired section of wire straight between your fingers and lay it in place to complete the wrap.

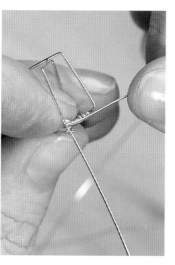

If you're working with a heavy wire that's too difficult to straighten by hand, or with a hard or short piece of wire, or if you need the wire to be perfectly straight, you will need to use tools to help you. In my opinion, the simplest method is to burnish the wire on a steel block. Hold the wire on top of the block so it's curving downward and rub it firmly with a burnisher. Rotate the wire, and continue rubbing and pushing until the wire is straight. Flip the wire and repeat

on the other end. This method is great for small pieces of wire and depends on the size of your steel block.

For all the projects in this book, using your fingers and the steel block/burnishing method will suffice.

Hardening Wire

In many situations you can harden wire by using the same techniques you'd use to straighten it. A good mantra to keep in mind is "metal hardens metal," which means that you'll want to use tools to get the strongest results. For my scale of work and for the projects in this book, you'll do most of your wire hardening by using a burnisher and steel block.

As mentioned above, burnishing on a steel block can harden metal. To see significant results, though, you must burnish aggressively, which can be exhausting. If you need to make a piece really hard, it's great to hammer it with a metal planishing hammer. If you want your design to have a flattened or hammered look, pound away (follow the technique described on pages 26 and 27). However, if you're hardening a pin stem or any type of post that you don't want to flatten, use a very gentle touch and keep the hammer and the post moving constantly to get allover, even coverage with little marking. Then follow up by burnishing to smooth out any marks, straightening the piece, and giving it a final hardening touch.

Bending Wire

Bending wire is pretty easy, but the tricky part is bending it where you want it to go! Most of the bending I do is with chain-nose pliers and my hands. Sometimes the pliers hold the wire while I bend with my fingers, and sometimes the other way around.

Whenever you work with chain-nose pliers, get a firm grasp on the wire but not so firm that you create an indentation in the wire. To avoid making marks, you can wrap the jaws of the pliers with masking tape or use pliers with nylon jaws, but if wire wrapping is your passion, you should learn a firm but gentle hold. Plus, you'll want the precision offered by unaltered pliers. Reposition your pliers if you feel them starting to slip. It's always better to let go of the wire than to hear the sharp snapping sound of jaws meeting after the wire has slipped out—that sound indicates that you've created a sharp burr and weakened the wire. Sometimes the wire can be salvaged by sanding it, but not often.

Making Sharp Bends

You'll use your hands and pliers together to make angled bends in the wire. For a 90°-angle bend, I position my chain-nose pliers and then use my fingers to push the wire so that it folds flat along the jaws to create the bend.

Sometimes a piece is designed in a way that makes it difficult to position the pliers properly, making it hard to form a sharp bend. In this case, I grasp the loose end of the wire in the pliers and give it a twist to make the bend. This is an imprecise method and should only be used in special cases since it doesn't yield a sharp bend.

If the bend is required on top of a bead or coil, I form the bend by pushing the wire flat against that object so that the bend conforms as closely as possible to the shape of the object.

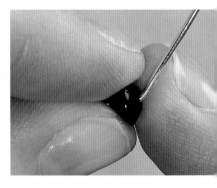

All of these techniques work for other angles as well. As you practice bends, you'll notice that thinner wires bend more sharply and that different types of wires respond differently.

Making Soft Bends

A common bend that I employ is the soft bend—or *kink*. I use kinks in two different ways. One is to mark a point where two wires cross and must realign.

The second way I use kinks is to add interest to or position beads on a wrapping wire.

Both types of kinks are made with a gentle motion. Grasp the wire in chain-nose pliers and twist your wrist gently to bend the wire where you want it. If you are positioning beads on wrapping wires, make the kink sharp enough to prevent the beads from sliding over it, but don't squeeze too hard or over-bend the wire so that it snaps.

Most of my wire wrapping is free-form, so I do virtually all of my bending as described above. Occasionally, though, you'll need a specific shape, in which case you can form the wire over anything. I use permanent markers and round pencils for ear hooks, and many rounded objects help me with curvilinear shapes. In general, don't be tempted to use your round-nose pliers for these shapes; reserve them almost exclusively for forming loops. Using round-nose pliers to make these kinds of bends will indent the wire and will ultimately create weak spots.

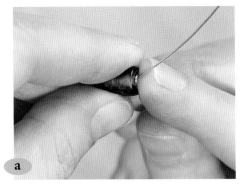

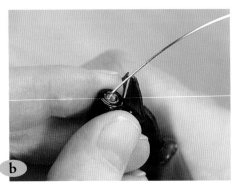

Forming Simple Loops

Making simple loops is an essential technique to master. These loops are fairly easy to create, but everyone has his or her own method for making them. Mine follows.

Use chain-nose pliers (or your finger, if necessary) to bend the wire at a 90° angle (photo a). Use wire cutters to flush cut the tail to ⅜ inch (1 cm) or to the desired length of the loop (photo b). (I refer to this as "loop length" in the project instructions.) Point the tail toward you and grasp its very tip in round-nose pliers, roughly centering it on the jaws with your palm facing away from you. Rotate your wrist forward while simultaneously pulling the wire taut and curling it (photo c). Don't torque your wrist; reposition the pliers and repeat the motion until the loop meets the 90° bend. To close the loop totally and center it, you can make final adjustments with chain-nose pliers (photo d). Use the opening/closing technique described on page 21.

Loop-Forming Tips

- It's better to form a loop that's too large for the piece of wire than too small. It's easier to create a smaller loop and cut off the excess wire.

- When I'm making the initial curl, I often position the wire closer to the base of the pliers in order to get a real curve. It's hard to grasp the very tip of the wire, but unless that part is curved, your loop will be teardrop shaped rather than round.

- You need only grasp the wire firmly in the beginning. When repositioning the pliers, try not to create any indents in the wire.

- Make any loop adjustments with chain-nose pliers.

- My most common tail length for a loop is ⅜ inch (1 cm), but heavy wires may need to be longer. You'll also need to gauge your loop size to accommodate any cords or other items that you'll be passing through the loop.

Forming Wrapped Loops

Wrapped loops are wonderfully secure links. They are formed in a slightly different manner than simple loops.

To make a wrapped loop, you should have at least 3 inches (7.6 cm) of wire to work with. Create a stem by grasping the wire with chain-nose pliers (photo a) and pushing the wire over the top of the pliers to form a 90° angle. Use round-nose pliers to grasp the wrapping wire (not the stem) at the 90° angle you just formed, positioning the wire on the pliers so that you'll end up with the size of loop you want (photo b). Hold the round-nose pliers in position while using your hand to pull the wrapping wire tightly over the top of the pliers until the wire is looped fully around and crosses the stem perpendicularly. Use chain-nose pliers to grasp the loop flat in its jaws and gently kink the wrapping wire where the wrapping should begin. If you are adding a link to this loop, slide it on now.

Once again grasp the loop flat in the chain-nose pliers and use your hand to tightly wrap the wire around the stem so it looks like a coil (photo c). Make two or more rotations to cover the stem and use wire cutters to flush cut the wire close to the coil (photo d). Grasp the coil flat in the jaws of flat- or chain-nose pliers and rotate the pliers in the direction of the coil, curving the tail over to tuck it in. You can give the tail a gentle squeeze if necessary, but be sure not to squeeze it so hard that it pops back out (photo e).

Coiling and Wrapping

When you make wrapped loops (see page 19), you can stabilize the wire by using one hand to hold onto the loop with pliers while you use your other hand to wrap the wire around itself. This setup makes it relatively easy to produce a tightly stacked coil. In other wrapping situations, such as ending a complex frame, you'll need to position your chain-nose pliers so they stabilize the frame as you pull the wire around the stem. In this type of situation, you probably won't be able to pull hard enough to form a tight coil (you don't want to distort your frame). Instead, start coiling the wire in position, and when it's secure and won't unwind, let go of the frame. Next, use chain-nose pliers to grasp the entire coil and rotate the pliers in the direction of the wrapping. When the wire is tight, hold the coil base and continue coiling if more rotations are desired or simply flush cut and finish it as described above.

When you need to attach one piece of wire to another—for example, a wrapping wire to a frame—wrap the wire loosely around the frame rib, leaving a tail to hold onto (photo a). Tighten the initial wrap with chain-nose pliers by gently squeezing it around the frame rib (photo b) and aligning the wires in a tight coil configuration (photo c); then hold onto the tail if more coils are desired (photo d). When you want to trim the initial tail, hold the wrapping wire to position the coil and keep it from spinning while you tighten and tuck it into place (photo e).

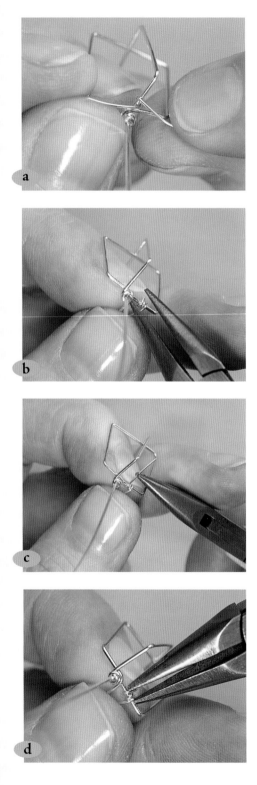

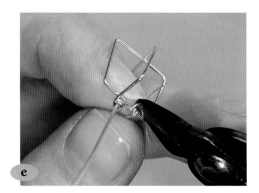

Opening and Closing Loops

To open and close loops, always use flat- or chain-nose pliers. The key is to twist the loop open to the side, creating a gap in the circle but without distorting the circle's shape or unwinding the loop (photo a).

Closing requires the same twisting motion and often feels like pushing the open side back into alignment. I usually grab the open edge, push/twist it into place, and then gently push it to either side of the center stem until it aligns perfectly in the center (sometimes it's hard to do this in one motion) (photo b). With heavy loops, you may have to hold the other side of the loop stable with another pair of flat- or chain-nose pliers.

a

b

Making a Basic Hook-and-Eye Clasp

You can purchase hook-and-eye clasps from a bead shop or craft store, but you may want to make your own. This type of clasp is great to use for the projects in this book, and because it's so easy to make, can easily be adapted to fit the style of whatever piece you're creating. Try working the teardrop end into a spiral, making the hook into an exaggerated shape, or playing with textures. The hook works especially well if it's made with 18-gauge or heavier wire and can be made from a variety of wires because the hammering hardens it.

First, use wire cutters to flush cut one end of a 3-inch (7.6 cm) piece of wire. Curl this end around the tip of round-nose pliers to start a loop shape (photo a). Push the loop flat toward the wire tail to create a teardrop shape (photo b). Form a hook by placing the base of the round-nose pliers about ¼ inch (.6 cm) from the tip of the teardrop. Wrap the wire around the pliers so it loops over and touches the teardrop (photo c). The cut end of the teardrop should be exposed on the outside edge of the loop.

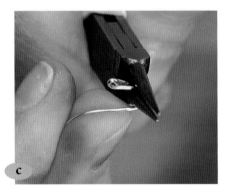

Use round-nose pliers to grasp the base of the hook just below where it touches the teardrop. Position the pliers so the wire is about midway down the jaws. Wrap the wire around the outside of the pliers until it crosses perpendicularly to the hook (photo d). Use the wire cutters to flush cut the wire at this point (photo e). Use chain-nose pliers to move the loop into place so the cut edge and hook meet flush.

Use a small file to taper the teardrop's cut edge and sand it smooth (see page 13).

To hammer the hook flat, hold the teardrop and the loop tightly together with your fingers and position the hook bend on a steel block (photo f). Hammer the top of the loop, flip it over, and repeat on the other side. Place the whole hook on the steel block. Continue holding the loop and teardrop together to prevent the hook from being distorted, while hammering down the sides of the hook gently so it tapers off smoothly where the wire rounds for the loop and teardrop. Flip the loop over and repeat. Photo g shows the same type of hook—one hammered, one not.

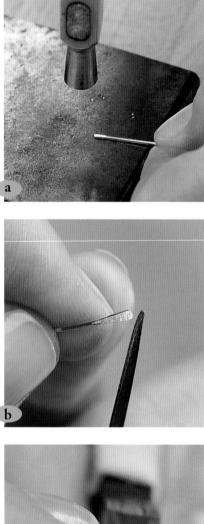

Making a Headpin

Headpins are straight pieces of wire that have a stopper at one end so beads don't fall off as you thread them on. They are most often used for making bead dangles. You can purchase headpins in all kinds of wire gauges, but sometimes it's easier to make your own. Here are two methods I use.

Select the gauge of wire that best fits your beads; 22- or 20-gauge wire works best. Use wire cutters to flush cut a piece of wire at least 2 to 3 inches (5 to 7.5 cm) long. Hold the flush-cut end of the wire on a steel block and hammer the end until it starts to flatten (photo a). Flip it over and hammer the other side until the end is a flat paddle. Finish the flattened paddles with a needle file and sandpaper (see page 13) so that no sharp edges remain and the shape is what you want (photo b).

You can also make simple headpins by using chain-nose pliers to fold the tip of a piece of 24- or 22-gauge wire back on itself, and then squeezing the fold flat (photos c and d). This is a great method for people who only have the Basic Tool Kit.

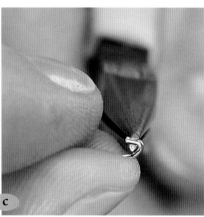

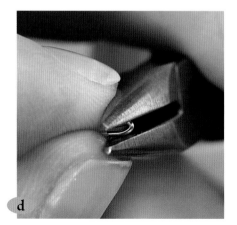

Purchasing Commercial Findings

If you're really into instant gratification, commercial findings can speed a project up. You can usually find a selection of basic clasps, headpins, and earring wires and posts at bead and craft stores. I have nothing against commercial findings unless they detract from the artistic vision of the piece. For a special gift or piece that you've put a lot of effort into, I generally recommend making the findings so that the whole piece has a handmade look.

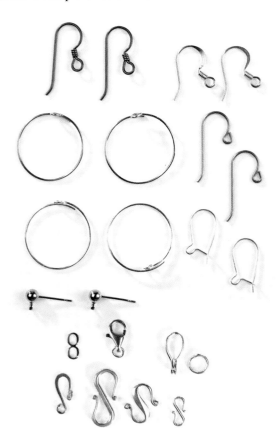

Changing the Look of Wire

Changing the surface appearance of wire adds a bit of mystery. Suddenly people aren't sure what type of metal they are looking at. For me it's especially fun to work with surface patinas such as liver of sulfur because it's hard to capture the exact same result every time—which in my mind makes a piece more artistic and special. Texturing also adds personality and can be altered not just by using different types and shapes of tools, but also by how the tools are held and by how much pressure is applied. Suddenly the possibilities seem endless.

Hammering Wire

Hammering wire is easy and can really change the look of a piece.

For basic flattening, hold the wire on a steel block and gently hammer it with a small planishing hammer. Flip the wire over and repeat on the other side. Continue flipping and adding more pressure to your hammering strokes until the wire is as flat as you want it. Be sure to hold the hammer as level as possible, or you will see hammer marks (photo a).

If you are hammering a shape or curve, try to hold the piece in such a way that you don't distort it as you hammer small sections and rotate it (photo b).

For complex shapes or spirals, I tend to hammer from the outside toward the inside, in the direction of the wrapping. If distortion happens, touch up the shape with flatnose pliers.

You don't need many tools to add texture; one or two hammers will do. Although this isn't required, I like to start by flattening my shapes or wires gently so I'll have a larger surface area for showing off the texture. Then I hammer with a texturizing hammer, using small deliberate strokes. Try a ball peen hammer for dimples, the tapered end of a riveting hammer for tiny lines, or the edge of a small hammerhead for larger, linear indents (photo c).

Oxidizing Wire

You can change the color of some wires by working with oxidizing agents—compounds that speed up the natural tarnishing process. These compounds are available through large jewelry suppliers and some craft stores.

Liver of sulfur is the oxidizing agent I use most often. It works on many different metals. I've had the most luck with sterling silver and copper, and it works subtly with brass, but it's ineffective with nickel silver, fine silver, and color-coated craft wires. A liver of sulfur solution turns silver black but can also bring out other colors, depending on how it's applied. My favorite method is to buy the dry compound (liver of sulfur comes in rocklike chunks) and mix a batch the size that I need. There's no set measuring method; I use a chunk in a small glass jar for small batches and several chunks in a large glass dish for bulk wire and larger pieces. I don't save my batches; I mix one fresh every time so it's as strong as possible. Stir the solution with a bamboo skewer or similar object; make sure to use only tools and containers dedicated for this use.

Liver of sulfur comes with mixing instructions, but I've found that using boiling water makes it much stronger and more dramatic. Experiment with dunking the wire quickly, at different areas on the same piece of wire, or for a longer period of time to see what colors develop. The colors that come out of sterling silver can be light gold; copper; burgundy; black with green, blue, or burgundy undertones; oil-slicked; or a totally flat gray.

Pliers can nick an oxidized finish, so oxidize your piece after all the bending is finished. If touch-ups are needed, dip a cotton swab or small paintbrush in the solution and apply the solution carefully.

You can change the look of a piece even more by following the oxidation with some of the finishing techniques described on page 28.

Finishes

You can apply a finish to a piece before, after, or instead of oxidizing. The easiest finish to apply, in my opinion, is a brushed finish. Brushed finishes can be done in a number of ways, and each has a slightly different look. You literally use a steel or brass brush designed for finishing purposes. Simply brush the object at all angles to create very tightly spaced, even scratches. The result is a subtle scratched surface that is still generally shiny.

For a more matte appearance, try rubbing the piece with an abrasive scouring pad. Hold the piece flat on some paper or another work surface, and apply firm pressure while rubbing in all directions. Pay attention to all the edges of the piece, especially if it's hammered. **Note**: You can get a similar texture by using steel wool, but it has a more random pattern, and I think it's much harder and unpleasant to work with.

If you want a more textured, reflective finish, try different grits of sandpaper. Rub the paper in one direction, in a circular motion or in a random pattern to get different looks. I usually go no lower than 220-grit because paper that's any rougher will create a texture that you can feel rather than just see—which is fine if that's what you're going for. For a very prominent finish, you can also use a flat or needle file.

The thing to keep in mind is to choose an appropriate texture for the piece. Don't overtexturize an ear wire or something that will touch your skin constantly. But do have fun playing around!

The Projects

Spiraling Charms

Simple spiral shapes are a snap to make!
Pair them with a purchased chain and wear
the bracelet tomorrow night.

what you will need

- 16-gauge brass wire, 18 inches (45.7 cm)
- 18-gauge nickel silver wire, 18 inches (45.7 cm)
- 16-gauge sterling silver wire, 18 inches (45.7 cm)
- 18-gauge gold-filled wire, 18 inches (45.7 cm)
- 20-gauge copper wire, 18 inches (45.7 cm)
- 18-gauge half-hard sterling silver wire, 3 inches (7.6 cm)
- Large-link chain, 7 to 8 inches (17.8 to 20.3 cm) or long enough to fit your wrist*
- Commercial clasp (optional)
- String
- Basic Tool Kit
- Planishing hammer
- Small ball peen hammer (optional)
- Other texturing hammers (optional)
- Steel block
- Liver of sulfur
- Burnisher

The easiest way to determine the length of large-link chain you'll need for your bracelet is to measure a bracelet you already have that fits well and subtract the length of the hook clasp. Alternatively, wrap a piece of string closely around your wrist. Add 1 inch (2.5 cm)—or any length that is comfortable and will allow for some movement— and subtract the length of the clasp.

getting started

Making spirals is easier when you work with a longer piece of wire than needed for the finished charm. The extra wire provides something to hold onto while you're doing the wirework. For these spirals, use the full 18-inch (45.7 cm) length of wire to begin the charm, ending the spiral when you feel it is the right size for your bracelet. Each piece of wire yields about four 3/4-inch-wide (1.9 cm) charms, but you can choose to make smaller or larger spirals as you wish.

making the round spiral charms

1 Use wire cutters to flush cut the tip of one of the lengths of wire. Use round-nose pliers to form a small simple loop at this end and tighten it with chain-nose pliers.

2 Use your dominant hand and chain-nose pliers to grasp the wire so the loop lies flat within the jaws. Position the loop so the point at which the wire touches itself sticks out slightly from the jaws. The long end of the wire should point away from your dominant hand.

To begin a spiral, firmly squeeze the loop and use your nondominant hand to bend the wire tightly but gently along the loop (photo a).

Reposition the pliers so the edge of the spiral lies at the edge of the jaws. Bend the wire as before, gently but tightly curving the wire along the spiral with your nondominant hand (photo b).

Tips

To create a tight spiral with minimal gaps, pull the tail of the wire very tightly so it touches the exposed part of the spiral. You may need to use your chain-nose pliers to keep the spiral together as you continue wrapping. For a more open spiral, don't pull the tail as tight, and adjust the position of the pliers more frequently.

Spiraling Charms

3 Create as many or as few turns as you wish. When you're finished, use the chain-nose pliers to bend the wrapping end of the wire to a 90° angle, straight up from the spiral (photo c). Then, bend the wire 90° perpendicular to the spiral and use round-nose pliers to form a simple loop (see page 18).

Tips

You may use this same spiraling technique to create oval shapes. Simply manipulate the wire differently, periodically squeezing the sides tightly with flat-nose pliers.

making the geometric spiral charms

1 Start the center loop as before, but this time use chain-nose pliers to bend a small version of the shape you wish to create (photo d). It may be difficult to form the precise shape, particularly with heavy-gauge wire, but after one tight bend has been established, you'll be able to start making the exact geometric form by holding the wrapping wire tightly at the desired bend point and pushing the wire over it to form a sharp bend (photo e). Continue spiraling out in this manner. Try squares, rectangles, and triangles.

2 You can also change the look of a shape by positioning the hanging loop in a different spot on the form (for example, by placing the loop in the corner of a square to make a diamond), as well as by varying the openness of the wrapping and the number of rotations.

making the triple circle cluster

1 Use wire cutters to flush trim the very end of the wire. Grasp the trimmed end with round-nose pliers, positioning the end on the portion of the jaws that will make your desired loop size. Pull the wire around the outside of one jaw until it meets the cut edge (photo f).

2 Reposition the pliers so one jaw is inside the loop and the other grasps the wrapping wire at the point where it meets the cut edge. Pull the wrapping wire around the outside of the jaw until it meets the other side of the first loop (photo g).

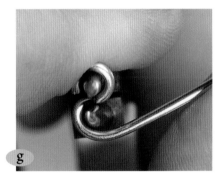

g

3 Insert one of the jaws into the first loop again, with the other jaw grasping the wrapping wire where it meets the outer edge of this loop. Let the loops stack while you wrap. Pull the wrapping wire around the outside of the jaw until it crosses the center point to form a sideways figure eight with the second loop. The first loop is centered below these two (photo h).

h

4 Use chain-nose pliers to align and flatten the shape.

5 Use the chain-nose pliers to grasp the wrapping wire at the center point and make a 90° bend (photo i). Then, bend the wire 90° perpendicular to the cluster (photo j). Use wire cutters to trim the wire and round-nose pliers to form a simple loop.

i

j

Spiraling Charms

planning the bracelet

1 Make a selection of charm shapes with each type of wire. You'll need enough charms to add one shape to each link of your chain. Be sure to leave the last link on each end of the chain open for the clasp.

2 Check all of the cut edges of the charms to make sure they are smooth. File and sand any rough edges (see page 13).

3 Add any desired finishes to the chain. Use the planishing and other texturizing hammers and the steel block to vary the finishes of the charms (see page 26), and apply any finishes to them that you like (see pages 27 and 28).

finishing up

1 Add the charms to the bracelet links one by one, using chain-nose pliers to open a top loop, passing it through a link on the chain, and closing the loop securely. Vary the positions of shapes, types of wires, and finishes.

2 Use the silver wire to make a hook-and-eye clasp (see page 22). If you don't wish to make your own, use a purchased clasp to finish the bracelet.

3 Add the hook to one end of the chain link. Secure the bracelet by fitting the hook through the last open link on the opposite end of the chain.

exploring the possibilities

What a difference scale makes! Try making mini charms all out of sterling silver, perhaps as a gift for a more conservative friend who loves your artistic side, but needs something that's comfortable under a suit jacket.

Spiral Scatter Pins

One would spark up a hat or tie, but why not make several and scatter them across a bare lapel?

Spiral Scatter Pins

what you will need

- 18-gauge half-hard sterling silver wire, 5 inches (12.7 cm) per pin
- 24-gauge half-hard sterling silver wire, 10 inches (25.4 cm) per pin for beaded option
- Selection of small stone, pearl, or glass beads for beaded option
- Tie tack clutch
- Basic Tool Kit
- Steel block
- Planishing hammer
- Burnisher

getting started

For stability reasons you'll want to keep these pins small, about a 1/2-inch (1.3 cm) diameter or smaller is best. Make a bunch of pins and group them together for the greatest visual impact.

making the spiral

1 Use wire cutters to flush trim each end of the 18-gauge wire.

2 Use chain-nose pliers to bend the 18-gauge wire at a 90° angle 3/4 inch (1.9 cm) from one end. This will become the pin stem (photo a).

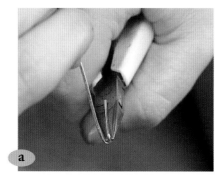

3 Hold the bend with chain-nose pliers as you start spiraling the wire in a circular direction, perpendicular to the pin stem. This is difficult to do, and you want these first spirals to be tight, so use flat-nose pliers to help grasp the wires as needed (photo b).

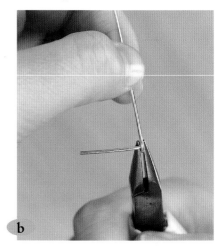

Note: For a different shape, start the center the same way as described in step 2. once you've established the first tight wrap, you can start bending linear geometric forms (triangle, diamond, square) with chain-nose pliers.

4 Once the center is established, keep holding the spiral flat between the pliers in one hand as you curve the wire around with the other hand to form a smooth spiral. Finish spiraling once you reach the desired size. Don't cut the excess wire.

hammering the shape

1 Use the tail to hold the spiral flat on a steel block with the pin stem pointing down along one side. Use the planishing hammer to hammer the top of the spiral, working from the outside in and following the direction of the wrapping. Rotate the top as you're working to fully hammer it.

2 Use chain-nose pliers to tighten or adjust the spiral if any warping occurred while hammering. Use round-nose pliers to form the tail into a loop to hang beads from. Simply bend the wire perpendicular to the shape, flush cut the wire, and form a simple loop that closes at the back.

finishing the pin

1 Straighten the pin stem by burnishing it on a steel block (see page 15). Use chain-nose pliers to adjust the bend position if needed.

2 Use wire cutters to flush cut the stem to 3/8 inch (1 cm). File and finish to a sharp point as shown on page 13.

3 Apply any finishing techniques as shown on pages 27 and 28. If you are making a beaded version, make your own headpins (see page 24) and attach beads with wrapped loops (see page 19). Cap the end with a tie tack clutch.

exploring the possibilties

Dangling beads not your cup of tea? Try using found objects instead of beads. If you have to have a simple tie tack or sedate lapel pin without dangling beads, cut the wire tail after you finish hammering your pin. Be sure you position your wire cutters at an angle so it will be easy to file the end into a smooth taper.

Silver Tendril Earrings

These simply elegant earrings will set your head spinning with possibilities for creative play.

what you will need

- 20-gauge half-hard sterling silver, two 5-inch (12.7 cm) pieces
- 2 sterling silver headpins, commercial or handmade (see page 24)
- 2 matching 4 to 6 mm beads to fit on the wire
- Basic Tool Kit
- Round pen, pencil, or dowel, from ¼ to ½ inch (.6 to 1.3 cm) in diameter
- Steel block
- Planishing hammer

making the spirals

1 Use wire cutters to flush trim the tip of one of the pieces of 20-gauge wire. Use round-nose pliers to create a small loop on the trimmed end and tighten the loop with flat-nose pliers.

2 Use your dominant hand and chain-nose pliers to grasp the wire so the loop lies flat within the jaws. Position the loop so the point at which the wire touches itself sticks out slightly from the jaws. The long end of the wire should point away from your dominant hand. (See page 30, Spiraling Charms, for photos of making spirals.)

Begin a spiral by firmly squeezing the loop and using your nondominant hand to bend the wire tightly but gently along the loop.

Reposition the chain-nose pliers so the edge of the spiral lies at the edge of the jaws. Bend the wire as before, gently but tightly curving the wire along the spiral with your nondominant hand.

Note: To create a tight spiral with minimal gaps, pull the tail of the wire very tightly so it touches the exposed part of the spiral. You may need to use your chain-nose pliers to keep the spiral together as you continue wrapping.

For a more open spiral, don't pull the tail as tight, and adjust the position of the pliers more frequently.

3 Create as many turns as you want, leaving at least 2 inches (5.1 cm) to form the ear hook. Set the spiral aside.

4 Repeat steps 1 through 3 to make a second spiral. The coils of the two spirals may not look exactly the same, but do your best to get a close match in diameter so the two are more or less the same size.

making the ear hooks

1 Hold a spiral so the wire tail points away from you. Position a round pencil next to the tail above the spiral. The pencil should sit on the side of the wire opposite the spiral (photo a). Wrap the tail over and around the pencil to form the ear hook.

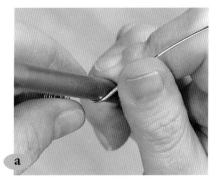

a

Silver Tendril Earrings

If the spiral and ear hook twists away use your fingers to adjust them so it is fairly flat again.

2 Use wire cutters to flush cut the wire tail even with the base of the spiral or to your desired length. Use chain-nose pliers to add a slight kink near the end of the ear hook to help prevent them from sliding out of your earlobes (photo b).

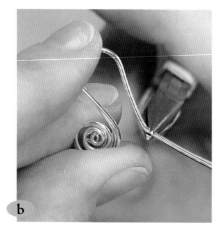

b

3 Hold the top of the spiral and the ear hook firmly with one hand on a steel block. Use a planishing hammer to gently hammer the bottom of the spiral. Continue to reposition the earring so you can hammer the spiral in the direction of the wrapping. To minimize distortion, hammer the entire spiral evenly, from the outside to the inside, always holding the ear hook in place with your hand (photo c).

4 Hold the bottom of the spiral and the end of the ear hook. Hammer along the ear hook between the spiral and the hook, up to the point where the hook would meet your earlobe (photo d).

c

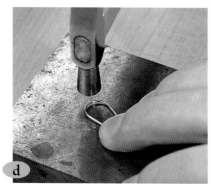

d

Flip the earring over and hammer the other side in the same manner. Repeat until the earring is completely flat.

5 Repeat steps 1 through 4 to make the second earring. Compare the two earrings and use chain-nose pliers to make any minor shape adjustments.

finishing up

1 File and sand the ends of the hook (see page 13).

2 Finish the earrings as desired (see pages 27 and 28). The earrings shown were brushed with an abrasive scouring pad to create an even, matte finish.

making the dangles

1 Use chain-nose pliers to hold the top of the spiral flat, positioning the hook outside the jaws. If you made a tight spiral, gently pull the interior spiral wraps up toward the top of the hook to create a gap at the bottom of the spiral; this gap will provide space for your dangle. If you created an open spiral, gently wiggle the spiral so the gap between the hook and the spiral is eliminated and your dangle won't slide off. Set the spiral aside.

2 Use one headpin to thread one bead, then make a simple or wrapped loop (see pages 18 and 19). Slide the dangle onto one of the ear hooks and down to the bottom of the spiral. Reposition and tighten the spiral as necessary so the dangle won't slide off.

3 Repeat steps 1 and 2 to add a dangle to the second earring.

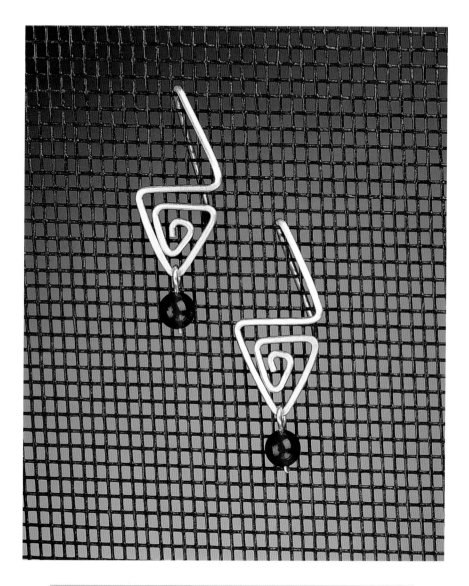

exploring the possibilities

Why be limited by circular spirals? Try your hand with other geometric forms or have fun making freeform spirals of your own design. Don't forget to play with scale… these earrings are fun small or large, and you can use any type of bead for a dangle.

Haywire Bangles

Once you've mastered these circular bangles, expand your design vocabulary with other shapes. Go haywire with ovals, squares, or triangles!

what you will need

- 20- or 18-gauge half-hard sterling silver wire, 4 to 5 feet (1.2 to 1.5 m) for each bangle*
- 24-gauge gold-filled wire for contrast wraps and embellishments
- Basic Tool Kit
- Strip of paper, 1 inch (2.5 cm) wide by 11 inches (27.9 cm) long
- Tape
- Liver of sulfur

Any metal will work well for this project, depending on the look you want. Sterling silver, steel, gold-filled, copper, and brass wire are all good choices, but if you have sensitive skin, stick with sterling silver or gold-filled wire.

sizing a bangle

1 Curl the paper strip into a circle that slides snugly over your hand. Tape it closed at that point. You'll use this paper circle as a general size template while forming the wire into a bangle.

forming the bangle

1 Use wire cutters to flush trim the tips of the sterling silver wire. Hold the wire 2 to 3 inches (5.1 to 7.6 cm) from one end. With your other hand, bend the long end of the wire to form a rough circle the same circumference as the paper template. When it's about the right size (err on the larger side, not on the smaller), use one hand to hold the wire circle together while using the other hand to twist the short tail around the circle.

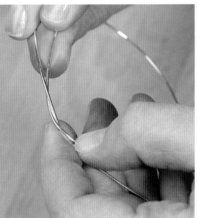

Let go of the long, loose end. Hold the bangle's shape, and tighten the tail wrap by cutting it close and tightening it with chain-nose pliers. Be sure to position the cut end so it faces away from the wrist. This is the bangle frame.

2 Hold the frame in one hand while passing the loose wire end through the center opening and around the frame with your other hand. Repeat all around the frame. The wrapping can be fairly loose to create free-form gaps, but pull the wire tighter every 2 to 3 inches (5.1 to 7.6 cm) to add some structure. For a more free-form look, position the tight wraps in different spots, and force the looser wraps to pop up in different points on the inside and outside of the bangle frame.

3 Continue wrapping until you are left with about 3 inches (7.6 cm) of loose wire. End the wire by wrapping it around just one of the wires in the bangle. Use chain-nose pliers to get a tight double wrap and use wire cutters to flush cut the wire close to the bangle. Use chain-nose pliers to tuck the tail into the wire wrapping.

4 Sand or file any exposed wire ends so they are smooth to the touch (see page 13).

finishing up

1 You can leave the bangle as is, or apply any finishes as desired (see pages 27 and 28).

2 Embellish your bangle with 24-gauge wire wraps (work with a contrasting color or finish). Try a variety of techniques: make tight or open coils, wrap around the full bangle width at various points, or coil around individual wires.

Cirque Ensemble

Why stop at only three rings? These rings are so easy to create that you'll want to make many more. Combine rings with the casual elegance of silk ribbon, cord, or chain, then top off the ensemble with a pair of earrings.

Necklace

what you will need

- 24-gauge gold-filled wire, 8 to 9 feet (2.4 to 2.7 m)
- Several 2 to 4 mm pearls or semi-precious stone, glass, or pearl beads to fit on the wire
- ½-inch-wide (1.2 cm) ribbon, 16 inches (40.6 cm) or any desired length
- 2 brass foldover ribbon crimps
- Gold-filled toggle clasp and jump rings
- Circle templates (optional)
- Basic Tool Kit
- Scissors
- Transparent tape

getting started

Designing a necklace is a personal process. Do you want a symmetrical or asymmetrical necklace? Do you want to graduate the sizes of your rings or make them all the same size? I make all of these rings free-form, but you can draw out templates for ring sizes if it makes the process easier for you.

These pieces begin with the same wrapping process used for the Haywire Bangles (on page 42), but this time you'll use a lighter gauge wire on a smaller scale.

To make the rings for this project, plan on using about 6 inches (15.2 cm) of wire for each small ring; about 10 inches (25.4 cm) for a medium ring; and about 15 inches (38.1 cm) for a large ring. I recommend working with extra wire—enough for two or three rings plus a couple of inches for easier manipulation and to cut down on waste.

making a beaded ring

1 To make a ring, start as if you were making a bangle. After the first wrap, the overall ring shape will need to be adjusted, especially at the spot where the wires cross and a point tends to form. To make the adjustment, use chain-nose pliers to lightly squeeze out any bumps in the shape until the ring is fairly circular.

2 Thread beads onto the wire between tight wraps. Vary the number of beads on each ring, and experiment with bead sizes and shapes to see how they change the appearance of the rings.

3 After two or three rotations (you may want to vary these numbers from ring to ring to create visual interest), wrap the tail around all of the wires in the ring. Use wire cutters to flush cut the wire and use chain-nose pliers to tuck the tail into the wrapping.

Cirque Ensemble

making the linked-ring chain

1 To create this necklace, you'll work from the sides toward the center. Start by making two rings with a 3/4-inch (1.9 cm) diameter. Set them aside.

2 Make two more rings with a 1-inch (2.5 cm) diameter. Set them aside.

3 Start one ring with a 7/8-inch diameter by using chain-nose pliers to lightly bend the two wires together to form little kinks where they cross rather than wrapping the tail. Open the wires at this point, and attach one large and one small ring.

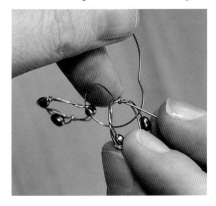

Hold the wires closed at the bend you made and proceed with wrapping the tail to completely close the ring. Make any corrections to the

ring shape, and wrap and add beads as usual, while rotating the ring so that the large and small rings hang freely out of the way at the bottom. When you finish the ring, you will end up with a three-link chain.

4 Repeat steps 1 through 3 to make another three-link chain.

Note: You can add one ring at a time in the same way, but it will take longer to form the whole chain this way. You may need to do this as you near the center of your necklace. Decide if you want an even (two joined rings sit at the center) or odd (one ring is centered) number of rings and how long you want the section of rings to be compared with the ribbon section.

5 Continue working toward the center of the necklace, gradually increasing the sizes of the rings, until you are forming the last ring where you join the two sides together to complete the chain. Using the specified amount of wire will allow you to make nine to ten rings.

finishing up

1 Decide what length of ribbon you want on each side to finish your necklace. Double the desired length and use scissors to cut two lengths of ribbon to that measurment.

2 Pass one ribbon length through one ring at the end of the chain. Pair the ribbon's ends and fold them together. Secure the fold with a tiny strip of tape no wider than the foldover crimp. Use scissors to trim any of the ribbon's frayed edges or loose strings.

3 To prepare the foldover crimps, use flat-nose pliers to grasp the top of one foldover edge and fold the crimp toward the center, leaving plenty of space for the ribbon end.

4 Slide the taped ribbon end under the partially-folded edge of the crimp. Be careful not to leave any ribbon peeking out at the top. Use flat-nose pliers to clamp the side of the crimp flat.

5 Use flat-nose pliers to grasp the top of the other edge of the foldover crimp and bend it toward the flattened one. Use flat-nose pliers to clamp the whole crimp flat.

6 Repeat steps 1 through 5 with the other side of the chain.

7 Use jump rings to attach each end of the toggle clasp to the ribbon.

Earrings

Now that you know how to make and join beaded rings of various sizes, you can design your own pair of earrings. Do you like small earrings with only one small ring, or do you like longer, dangly earrings with multiple rings of different sizes? Have fun experimenting. These instructions are for a triple-ring dangle to match the necklace.

- **24-gauge gold-filled wire, 2 feet (61 cm)**

- **Several 2 to 4 mm semiprecious stone, glass, or pearl beads to fit on the wire**

- **Gold-filled French ear wires**

- **Basic Tool Kit**

1 Make two three-link chains by following steps 1 through 4 in Making the Linked-Ring Chain (on page 46).

2 Use flat-nose pliers to open the loop on one of the earring findings, just as you would open a jump ring. Attach the loop to the smallest ring on one of the three-link chains and close the loop. If the entire ring width is too thick to fit in the finding's loop, simply hook one of the wires that makes up the ring onto the loop. Repeat with the other three-link chain.

Dancing Branches

Capture the appearance of buds on bare branches in spring with this delicate necklace that nestles on your collarbone.

Necklace

what you will need

- 24- or 22-gauge half-hard sterling silver wire (use the heaviest gauge that fits your beads), 3 feet (91.4 cm) for a 16 to 18 inch (40.6 to 45.7 cm) necklace
- 22-gauge half-hard or heavier sterling silver wire, approximately 6 inches (15.2 cm) for a handmade clasp
  or
  Commercial clasp
- Simple color palette of semiprecious stone, glass, or pearl beads in a variety of shapes, sizes, and finishes, to measure 15 inches (38.1 cm) in length
- Basic Tool Kit
- Beyond the Basics Tool Kit

getting started

When designing a fun, free-form necklace like this one, I don't make it from one end of the clasp to the other. I find it easier to achieve variety and randomness by thinking about the individual components. By concentrating on the individual necklace links rather than trying to conceptualize the entire piece, I can easily keep the aesthetic light and airy. Working this way is a good trick for fighting our natural tendency to make symmetrical patterns!

When making links, I prefer to mix up the lengths. I make short links—each 1/2 to 3/4 inch (1.2 to 1.9 cm)—to help smooth out the curve between some larger 1 1/2-inch (3.8 cm) links, and I add some sizes in between. (The link lengths are all approximate.)

making branch links

1 Make the small, simple links first. Use wire cutters to flush trim the tip of the 3-foot (91.4 cm) wire and form a simple loop at the trimmed end (see page 18). Thread a bead, and leaving some empty space on the wire, use wire cutters to flush cut the other end to loop length. Make a simple loop at this end perpendicular to the first loop.

2 Use chain-nose pliers to bend one or two kinks in the wire to position the bead where you want it—moved to one end or suspended in the middle (see page 17). Bend only enough to prevent the bead from sliding over the kink.

3 Repeat steps 1 and 2 to create six to eight simple links. Make each one slightly different from the others by varying the link length, bead type, and/or bead position. When planning your necklace, keep in mind that you'll need a couple of small bead links near the clasp and a few short links near the bends in the necklace, where it drapes around the neck.

4 Create larger links. These can each have only one large bead on its own or several beads, with kinks separating or grouping them. Have fun making a variety of simple combinations on each branch, such as one link with a small-large combination, one with a dark-light-dark combination, and another with a translucent-opaque combination. I find that focusing on the individual branches at this point and making each one different help me achieve a more random look.

5 When your branches are finished, connect them to one another. Use flat-nose pliers to open the simple loop at one end of the link (as you would a jump ring); attach the next link by passing one of its end loops over the first link's open loop; close the loop; and repeat. Start and end with the small bead links that will connect to the clasp. Again, try not to create a pattern—just link together what comes to hand.

6 When the branches reach your desired necklace length, hold the length in place around your neck, and check to see if you are pleased with the design and how it drapes. Reposition the branches as needed. For instance, if a heavy bead falls too close to the center and pulls the necklace in an awkward direction, move that branch farther away from the center. Or if a dark bead lands right in the center of the necklace, creating too much of a focal point, you may want to move the branch elsewhere.

making the ring for the hammered toggle clasp

1 Use wire cutters to flush trim the very ends of the 6-inch (15.2 cm) piece of wire. Use chain-nose pliers to bend a 90° angle about ¹/₂ inch from the end of the wire. This is the ring post.

2 Wrap the long, loose end into a small circle around a pencil or do it freeform around your pinky finger (photo a).

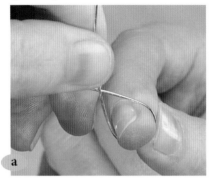

a

End the wrap by coiling it around the post twice (photo b). Use wire cutters to flush cut the wire and chain-nose pliers to tuck the tail. Bend the post so it is at a 90° angle directly on top of the coil. Use wire cutters to flush cut the wire to loop length and form a simple loop (see page 18) perpendicular to the clasp ring.

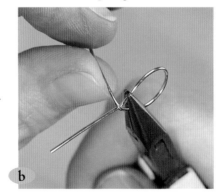

b

3 Use a planishing hammer and steel block to hammer the ring until it's slightly flattened and very firm (photo c). Finish as desired (see page 28).

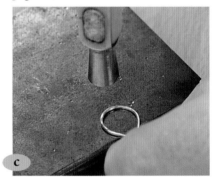

c

making the bar

1 Position round-nose pliers at the center of the remaining wire. Wrap each end of the wire halfway around the top arm of the pliers so they cross, forming a loop with a T above it (photo d).

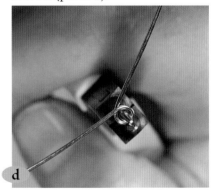

d

2 Hold the loop flat in the jaws of flat nose pliers and the T-wires firmly in your hand. Give the loop a full twist to close it (photo e). Use flat-nose pliers to square off the T-bars. Use wire cutters to flush cut the T-bars so they are each slightly longer than the ring's diameter (photo f).

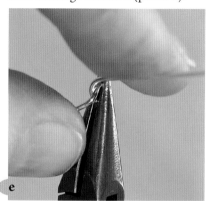

e

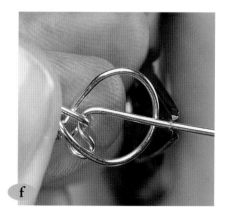

f

3 Use a planishing hammer and steel block to hammer the T-bars flat, ensuring that the flat edge is perpendicular to the loop (photo g).

g

File and shape (see page 13) the ends of the bar. Finish as desired.

finishing up

1 Use flat-nose pliers to open the available loops of the necklace's end links. Attach the clasp and close the loops. The necklace may be worn with the clasp in front or back.

Earrings

what you will need

- 26-, 24-, or 22-gauge half-hard sterling silver wire (use the gauge that best fits your beads), 8 inches (20.3 cm)

- Selection of semiprecious stone, glass, and/or pearl beads

- French ear wires or posts with hanging loops

- Basic Tool Kit

Dancing Branches

forming the branches

1 Use wire cutters to flush trim the tip of the wire. Use chain-nose pliers to grasp the trimmed end and fold the tip of the wire back on itself. Squeeze the fold flat so it's flush.

2 Thread the beads that you want to use for the longest branch onto the wire. Use chain-nose pliers to bend the wire at a 90° angle, about 1½ inches (3.8 cm) from the folded tip. Use wire cutters to flush cut the wire to loop length and round-nose pliers to form a simple loop (see page 18).

3 Repeat steps 1 and 2 to create the longest branch for the other earring. The two branches need to be the same length for visual balance but otherwise don't need to match.

4 Make two more branches for each earring in the same manner. Add one or two beads to each branch, but don't make exact matches. These branches can vary in length but should be shorter than the first branch.

finishing up

1 When all the branches are finished, space out the beads as desired by using chain-nose pliers to bend kinks in the wire, as in the necklace project above.

2 Use flat-nose pliers to open a loop on one of the earring findings, just as you would open a jump ring. Add one of the longest branches and two of the shorter branches in any order you desire. Close the loop. Repeat with the other earring finding.

exploring the possibilities

This set is easy to customize by choosing different color palettes for the stones. The variation shown captures the feeling of autumn with an orange-rust color palette that the warmth of gold-filled wire complements. Have fun playing with colors and stone shapes for your own special look.

For the necklace, you can also try making a different type of clasp, such as the twisted wire toggle clasp shown at right or a commercial clasp of your choice.

Hip 2 B Square Pin

Why knot a wrap or shawl? Use this graphic pin to
complete your outfit and make a bold statement.

Hip 2 B Square Pin

what you will need

- 22-gauge half-hard sterling silver wire, 6 feet (1.8 m)
- 26-gauge half-hard sterling silver wire, 1 foot (30.5 cm)
- 18-gauge nickel silver wire, 8 inches (20.3 cm)
- Glass bead to fit 18-gauge wire, at least 1 cm in diameter*
- Stick pin end cap (optional)
- Basic Tool Kit
- Liver of sulfur
- Burnisher
- Steel block
- Planishing hammer

*Choose a large bead to create a colorful finial for your pin stem.

forming the square

1 Use wire cutters to flush trim the tips of the 22-gauge wire. Use chain-nose pliers to bend a 90° angle, 2 inches (5.1 cm) from one end of the wire. Use your fingers to straighten the wire, removing any curves.

2 Bend another 90° angle in the wire, 2 inches (5.1 cm) from the previous bend, always smoothing the wire to remove any curves. Repeat until you've made a square.

3 Hold the square tightly with one hand as you continue to bend the wire to create a repeating square. Don't worry if the sides aren't exactly the same—that's the fun of making free-form shapes. If you need to let go of the square, restack the wire and hold it to maintain a loose square shape.

4 When you are satisfied with the thickness of your square (for the pin shown, I repeated the square shape eight or nine times), use wire cutters to flush cut the wire at the corner opposite to the one at which you started.

5 Hold the square on the side where you just made the cut. Use chain-nose pliers to bend the end of the wire back up so the end meets the center point of this side. Hold the square as firmly as possible and coil the wire tightly twice around the entire bundle of wires. Use wire cutters to flush cut the wire and use chain-nose pliers to tuck in the tail. Repeat this step on the opposite side with the beginning of the wire.

6 Apply any desired finishes (see pages 27 and 28).

7 Use wire cutters to flush cut a 6-inch (15.2 cm) length of 26-gauge wire. Starting close to the wrap you made in step 5, wrap one end of the 26-gauge wire twice around a single 22-gauge wire to secure the end (photo a).

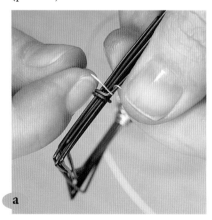

a

Use wire cutters to flush cut the 26-gauge wire and use chain-nose pliers to tuck the tail to the inside of the square. Wrap the 26-gauge wire fully around the 22-gauge bundle to conceal the initial wrapping from step 5 and to hide the starting coil of the 26-gauge wire (photo b).

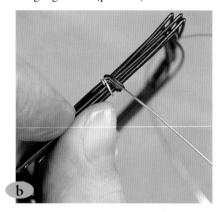

b

When you've concealed the wrapped bundle, wrap the tail around a single 26-gauge wire strand at the back (photo c). Use wire cutters to flush cut the wire and use chain-nose pliers to tuck the tail into the wire wrapping on the back of the pin.

c

8 Use the remaining 26-gauge wire to wrap the opposite bundle of 22-gauge wire on the other side of the square. Make sure that you tuck the tail at the back of the pin.

making the beaded pin stem

1 Thread the bead onto the nickel silver wire, leaving a 2-inch (5.1 cm) tail (photo d). Use chain-nose pliers to bend the short tail at a 90° angle. Hold the bead close to the angle and bend the longer wire at a 90° angle so the two wires are parallell (photo e).

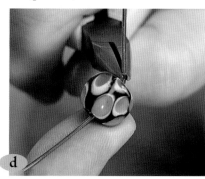

Bend both wires around the bottom of the bead (photo f).

Bend the longer wire at a 90° angle so it comes straight down from the center of the bead (photo g). Coil the shorter wire around this stem twice (photo h). Use wire cutters to flush cut the tail and chain-nose pliers to tighten the coil.

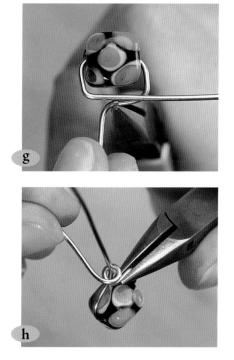

2 Use wire cutters to flush cut the wire approximately 4 inches (10.2 cm) down from the bead. File and finish this end to a sharp point (see page 13).

3 Use a burnisher to straighten the wire on a steel block. Use a planishing hammer and steel block to harden the pin stem by gently hammering it (see page 26).

4 If desired, cap the sharp end of the pin stem with an end cap.

5 To wear the pin, place the wire square on top of the fabric. Pull a little of the fabric through the center of the pin. Push the pin stem through the fabric from one side of the square to the other.

exploring the possibilities

Since this pin has a separate pin stem, you can create a whole wardrobe of pin stems. Using the same beaded version described here, try different bead shapes and colors to coordinate with different outfits. You could also make a pin stem that's capped with a wire orb (see page 67) for a neutral option that complements any wardrobe. Did you love the Spiraling Charms Bracelet on page 30? If so, try designing your own pin stem with a spiral finial. And remember you aren't limited to silver... explore types and colors of wire as well!

Bound Chaos Pendant

Sometimes it's all in the package. This little bundle of chaotic wire strands acts as a fanciful bow to set off the pearl.

what you will need

- 22-gauge half-hard sterling silver wire, 2 feet (61 cm)
- 24-gauge half-hard sterling silver wire, 18 inches (45.7 cm)
- 6 to 8 mm pearl bead
- Sterling silver headpin, commercial or handmade (see page 24)
- Sterling silver chain with clasp, 18 inches (45.7 cm) or any desired length
- Basic Tool Kit
- Liver of sulfur

bundling the wire

1 Use wire cutters to flush trim each end of the 22-gauge wire. Use chain-nose pliers to loosely fold the wire back on itself (don't flatten the sides together), about 1 inch (2.5 cm) from one end. Fold the end back on itself, again about 1 inch (2.5 cm) from the first bend (photo a).

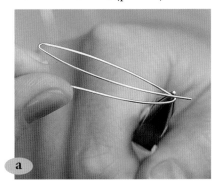

Continue bending the wire back and forth in this fashion. The bends don't have to be the same in length or perfectly aligned.

2 When the bundle is the size you desire (the bundle shown was bent about eight times on each side), find the starting tail and while holding the bundle together for stability, use chain-nose pliers to bend the tail at a 90° angle perpendicular to the bundle.

Wrap this tail once around the entire bundle (photo b). Use wire cutters to flush cut the wire and chain-nose pliers to tuck the tail into the wire wrapping.

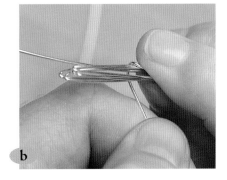

3 Repeat step 2 with the other end of the wire.

4 Oxidize the bundle with liver of sulfur (see page 27).

working the contrast wrapping

1 Use wire cutters to flush cut each end of the 24-gauge wire. Hold the wire perpendicular to the bundle on one side, leaving a 2-inch (5.1 cm) tail sticking out. Wrap the working end of the wire around the middle section of the bundle, completely covering the tails that secure the bundle.

2 Pass the wire under a few of the coils so the wraps are secure and the working wire is opposite the other tail (photo c).

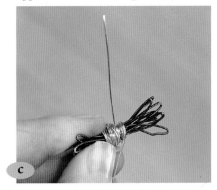

3 Form a wrapped loop with each tail (see page 19) so that you end up with one loop adjacent to the top and one loop adjacent to the bottom of the bundle. Make sure the top loop is wide enough to slip over the clasp. (You may also choose to put the pendant on the chain before wrapping the loop closed.)

finishing up

1 Use chain-nose pliers to separate and splay the bundle branches that stick out to either side. You can open the bends, add kinks, or do whatever you like to make an interesting shape.

2 Thread the bead onto the headpin and make a simple loop to secure it in place (see page 18). Use flat-nose pliers to open the simple loop, just as you would open a jump ring, and attach the loop to the wrapped loop at the bottom of the bundle.

3 Hang the pendant from the chain.

Amphora Necklace and Earrings

Here's a chance for you to be creative with simple, classical shapes or shapes of your own invention. This elegant amphora shape is filled with stones that pour onto the chain.

Amphora Necklace

what you will need

- 20-gauge half-hard sterling silver wire, 6 inches (15.2 cm)
- 26-gauge sterling silver wire, 1 foot (30.5 cm)
- Sterling silver link chain with clasp, 16 inches (40.6 cm) or any desired length
- 24-gauge half-hard sterling silver wire for bead links (optional)
- Semiprecious stone, glass, or pearl beads to fit on 26-gauge wire*
- Basic Tool Kit
- Simple wrapping forms (see page 10)
- Fine-point permanent marker
- Planishing hammer
- Steel block
- Burnisher
- Liver of sulfur (optional)

*2 to 3 mm beads are best for the pendant, but you can use larger ones for the chain links.

getting started

Select an amphora or vase-like shape to use as your central pendant. Look for shapes in design books, sketch out ideas, or simply start with a concept and see what happens with the wire as you work. The designs discussed in this project are all based on a pointed bottom.

The delicate lines of wire with beads dancing across them will connect the two sides of the amphora shape. The wires add beauty, and their tension also contributes both shape and structure.

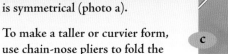

Making Complex Amphora Shapes

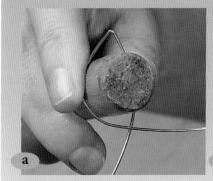

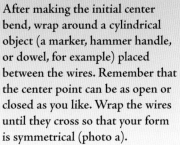

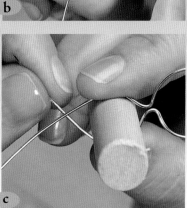

After making the initial center bend, wrap around a cylindrical object (a marker, hammer handle, or dowel, for example) placed between the wires. Remember that the center point can be as open or closed as you like. Wrap the wires until they cross so that your form is symmetrical (photo a).

To make a taller or curvier form, use chain-nose pliers to fold the wires back from each other (photo b) so that you can wrap around another object (photo c). *Note:* If you decide to make a large, more ornate shape, you'll need to begin with a longer piece of wire.

Amphora Necklace and Earrings

making the frame

1 Use wire cutters to flush trim each end of the 20-gauge wire. Using chain-nose pliers to hold the center of the wire, bend a 45° angle to create the amphora shape's base (photo a). Form the sides of the shape by pulling and curving the wire between your fingers, from the center point to the cut ends. *Note:* Because you're working with a 6-inch (15.2 cm) piece of wire, you have 3 inches (7.6 cm) on each side of the bend to form your amphora shape.

2 When you are pleased with your shape, use a ruler to measure the length of each side and use a fin-point permanent marker to mark the base of the loops that will connect to the chain. Use chain-nose pliers to bend the wire to a 90° angle at these marks (photo b). Use wire cutters to flush cut the wire to loop length and use round-nose pliers to form simple loops at each end of the wire (photo c). Position the loops to continue the line of your form as it connects to the chain.

3 To strengthen the frame, use a planishing hammer and steel block to gently tap the bent points and curves. You don't need to hammer the whole shape; just hammer the key points to add strength where the wire has been bent. Burnish the whole shape to harden the wire (see page 15).

4 Apply any desired finishes to the frames. *Note:* If you want to darken your piece, oxidize the frame as well as the wrapping wire and the chain before you add beaded wraps.

a

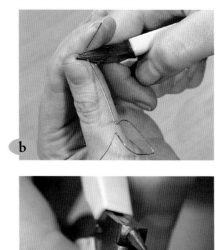
b

c

adding beaded wraps

1 Use chain-nose pliers to tightly wrap the end of the 26-gauge wire twice around one top side of the shape (photo d). Use wire cutters to flush cut the short tail and use chain-nose pliers to tuck the tail so that it sits neatly inside the frame. Gently

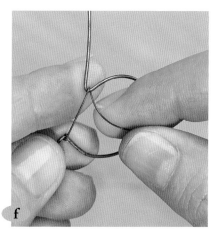

f

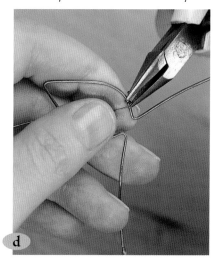

d

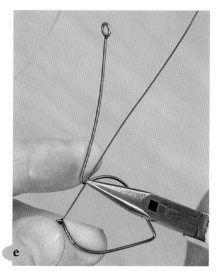

e

pull the wire across to the other side of the frame, holding the shape exactly the way you want it. Use chain-nose pliers to kink the wire at the wrap point (photo e) and wrap it once around the frame as you hold the shape and wrapping wire in place. This should establish and secure your form (photo f).

2 Thread one or two beads onto the wrapping wire and pull the wire across the frame. Wrap once around the other side so the wraps are tight but are far enough apart to allow the beads to slide around.

3 Continue wrapping and adding beads as you work toward the bottom tip. You'll need to hold the wraps in place and be careful not to pull too tightly, or the wires will slide down the form.

4 When you reach the tip, finish by wrapping twice around the frame. Use wire cutters to flush cut the wire and chain-nose pliers to tuck the tail so that it sits neatly inside the frame.

5 Use chain-nose pliers to add kinks to the wires and to position the beads as desired, leaving some space for the beads to slide (see page 17).

finishing up

1 Fold your chain in half and use wire cutters to cut the middle link so you end up with two lengths of chain.

2 Use flat-nose pliers to open the amphora's loops, just as you would open a jump ring. Attach one loop to the end link of one length of chain. Close the loop. Repeat with the other loop and length of chain.

3 For a more custom-made look, remove some chain links and insert wrapped loop bead links (see page 19) at random or regular intervals.

Amphora Necklace and Earrings

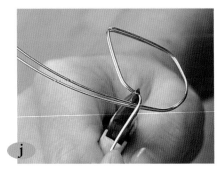

Amphora Earrings with

what you will need

- 20-gauge half-hard sterling silver wire, two 6-inch (15.2 cm) pieces
- 26-gauge sterling silver wire, 2 feet (61 cm)
- Several 2 to 3 mm semiprecious stone, glass, or pearl beads
- Basic Tool Kit
- Simple wrapping forms (optional)
- Large marker or dowel
- Planishing hammer
- Steel block
- Burnisher
- Liver of sulfur (optional)

making the earring frames

1 Use wire cutters to flush trim the tips of the 20-gauge pieces of wire. Use the chain-nose pliers to hold the two pieces of wire together at their midpoints. Bend a 45°-angle curve in both wires at the same time (photo g).

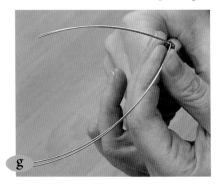

2 Form an amphora shape in the same manner as you did with the necklace pendant, working freehand or wrapping the wires around curved forms (photo h). It's important to form the earrings simultaneously by holding the wires together.

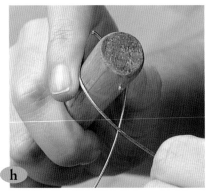

3 With the other wire ends, form the top hook portion of the earrings. Use your fingers to pull and form the front of the earring to the ear-hook point, then wrap the wires around the top of a large permanent marker or dowel until the wires (photo i).

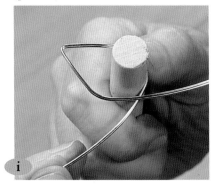

4 After you've established the frame's shape, use chain-nose pliers to bend one of the wire ends at a 90° angle away from the top of the amphora shape. This bend will ultimately form the hook catch (photo j).

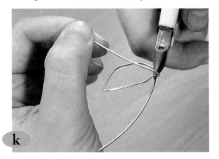

5 Working with one earring frame at a time, use chain-nose pliers to hold the 90°-angle tail at the bend. Wrap the tail around the pliers to form

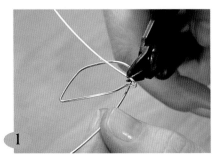

a hook perpendicular to the earring (photo k). Use wire cutters to flush cut the hook so that the end is parallel with the frame edge (photo l). Repeat for the other earring frame, making sure the hook wraps to the opposite side so that your earrings are mirror images of each other.

6 At this crossing point, use chain-nose pliers to add a small kink to the ear wires. Use wire cutters to flush cut these ends to the desired length, approximately ³/₈ inch (1 cm) from the kink just made (photo m).

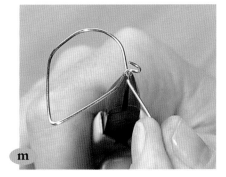

m

7 Use the planishing hammer to gently tap each earring on a steel block, especially the bottom point and front section of the ear hook to the point where it enters the ear. Burnish the whole shape to harden it (see page 15).

8 Finish all of the wire's cut ends, giving the ear hook a rounded tip (see page 13). Be sure to keep the catch loop flat.

9 Apply any desired finishes to the frames. *Note*: If darkening your piece, oxidize all of the frames as well as the wrapping wire.

adding beaded wraps

1 Use chain-nose pliers to tightly coil one end of the 26-gauge wire twice around one top side of the amphora shape, under the catch loop. Use wire cutters to flush cut the short tail and use chain-nose pliers to tuck the tail so that it sits neatly inside the frame. Gently pull the wire across to the other side of the frame, holding the shape exactly the way you want it. Use chain-nose pliers to kink the wire at the wrap point, and wrap it once around the frame as you hold the shape and wrapping wire in place. This should establish and secure your frame.

2 Thread one or two beads onto the wrapping wire and pull the wire across the frame. Wrap once around the other side so that the wraps are tight but far enough apart to allow the beads to slide around.

3 Continue wrapping and adding beads as you work toward the bottom tip. You will need to hold the wraps in place and be careful not to pull too tightly, or the wires will slide down the form.

4 When you reach the tip, end by coiling the wire twice around the frame. Use wire cutters to flush cut the wire and use chain-nose pliers to tuck the tail so it sits neatly inside the frame.

5 Use chain-nose pliers to add kinks to the wires, positioning the beads where you want them and leaving enough space for the beads to slide.

6 Adjust the ear wire by opening it wider to create tension in the catch hook.

7 Repeat steps 1 through 6 to finish the other earring.

exploring the possibilities

Try your hand at making curvier shapes as described on page 59. You can also play with scale, finish, and color. Make smaller or larger versions; try oxidizing the wire or keeping it shiny; or mix it up by using multiple wire colors for the wraps.

Bewitching Charm Necklace

You've learned to make simple shapes; now mix and match your own choices to create a one-of-a-kind necklace that will charm everyone.

- 22-gauge half-hard sterling silver wire, approximately 26 inches (66 cm)
- 26-gauge sterling silver wire, 3 feet (91 cm)
- Sterling silver chain with clasp, 18 inches (45.7 cm)
- 2 to 3 mm semiprecious stone, glass, or pearl beads to fit on 26-gauge wire
- Basic Tool Kit
- Fine-point permanent marker
- Simple wrapping forms (optional, see page 10)
- Planishing hammer
- Steel block
- Burnisher
- Liver of sulfur (optional)

getting started

The wire measurements listed are for five shapes from 1 to 2 inches (2.5 to 5.1 cm) in length. (All of the shapes are made using the one piece of 22-gauge wire.) Think in terms of organic, curvy shapes that contrast with some geometric forms. Also vary the length and width of each one to make them less uniform. I tend to work free-form, making whatever shapes come to mind and simply forming them with pliers. This makes the shapes slightly irregular and gives them more of a hand-drawn quality. You can also sketch shapes to use as templates (especially helpful for scale and sizing) or wrap the wire around a form to create the frame.

You can change the look of this piece greatly by using 20-gauge wire instead of 22-gauge wire for the frames. *Note:* When you're working with the heavier gauge, you only need to tap the curves in the frame rather than hammering the whole shape to add strength (see Making the Frames, step 5).

making the frames

1 Use wire cutters to flush trim the tips of the 22-gauge wire. Use chain-nose pliers to form a bend in the wire, 2½ to 3 inches (6.4 to 7.6 cm) from the end. Fold the wire ends toward each other to form the point of a long, thin triangle.

2 Use chain-nose pliers to bend the corners of the triangle about 1 to 1½ inches (2.5 to 3.8 cm) up from the point. Make these bends so they are at sharp angles to each other (photo a).

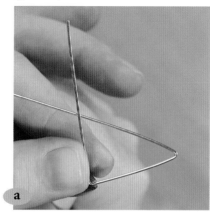

3 Use chain-nose pliers to form a post by bending the short tail at a 90° angle from the center top side (photo b). Bend the long tail at the angle just made. Coil the long tail around the post twice (photo c). Use wire cutters to flush cut the long tail and use chain-nose pliers to tuck it in.

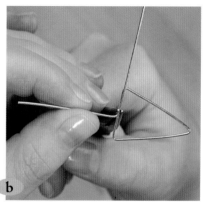

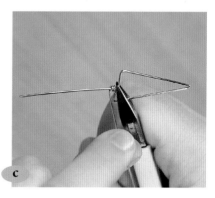

Bewitching Charm Necklace

4 Use chain-nose pliers to bend the exposed post wire at a 90° angle directly on top of the coil. Use wire cutters to flush cut the wire to a loop length and round-nose pliers to form a simple loop (see page 18). Make sure the loop is facing the right way for the shape to lie flat when it dangles from the chain.

5 To add strength, use a planishing hammer and steel block to gently hammer the entire shape. Do not flatten it.

6 Repeat steps 1 through 5 to make a selection of shapes. For a more random look, vary the lengths and types of the shapes, making them as geometric or curvilinear as desired.

7 Apply any desired finishes to the frames. **Note:** If darkening your piece, oxidize all of the frames as well as the wrapping wire and the chain.

wrapping the shapes

1 Use chain-nose pliers to tightly coil the end of the 26-gauge wire twice around one top side of the shape. Use wire cutters to flush cut the short tail and chain-nose pliers to tuck in the tail so it sits neatly inside the frame. Gently pull the wire across to the other side of the frame. **Note:** The closed, flat shapes can be awkward to stop and start. Just remember that you are in control and place the wire where you want it.

2 Thread one or two beads onto the wrapping wire, pull the wire across the frame, and wrap it once around the other side. These side wraps should be tight but not so closely spaced that the beads can't slide around.

3 Continue wrapping and adding beads as you work toward the bottom tip. You'll need to hold the wraps in place and be careful not to pull too tightly, or the wires will slide down the form.

4 When you reach the tip, end by coiling the wire twice around the frame. Use wire cutters to flush cut the wire and chain-nose pliers to tuck in the tail so that it sits neatly inside the frame.

5 Use chain-nose pliers to add kinks to the wires (see page 17) and to position the beads where you want them, leaving enough space for the beads to slide.

finishing up

1 Use flat-nose pliers to open the loop on the charm that you'd like to place at the middle of the chain, just as you would a jump ring. Attach the loop to the middle link on the chain and then close the loop. Continue adding charms in this manner, working from the center outward. Count the links between charms to achieve even spacing.

Celestial Orbit Pendant and Earrings

If you've ever wound a ball of yarn, you're ready for this project. Suspend this wire orb on ribbon, cord, chain, or whatever your heart desires.

Celestial Orbit Pendant and Earrings

Pendant

what you will need

- 20-gauge colored craft wire, 2 feet (61 cm)
- Ribbon, 16 to 18 inches (40.6 to 45.7 cm) or any desired length
- 2 foldover ribbon crimps
- Clasp
- Basic Tool Kit

getting started

To understand the process and the tension involved, practice making a ball or two with inexpensive wire. Once you've got the process down, move on to more expensive wire and have fun!

You'll use the following directions in any project using wire orbs.

forming a ball

1 Use wire cutters to flush trim the tips of the wire. Use chain-nose pliers to form a teardrop shape approximately ⅛ inch (3 mm) long at one end of the wire. *Note:* For a larger ball, start with a larger teardrop; use a smaller teardrop to make a smaller ball.

2 At the point where the cut end meets the loose wrapping wire, use chain-nose pliers to bend the wrapping wire at a 90° angle (photo a).

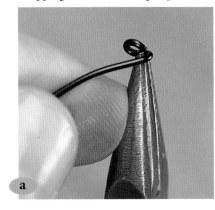

Hold the wire close to this bend with the pliers and use your thumb to push the wire gently so it encircles the teardrop loosely (photo b).

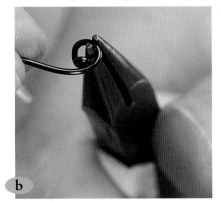

3 Keep working the wire around the center, changing the direction of the wrapping to form a sphere, as if you were winding a ball of yarn (photo c). In general, the ball should not be wrapped too loosely. You want to achieve some airiness, but for stability, the wrapping wire should touch the wires of the spherical core at some points.

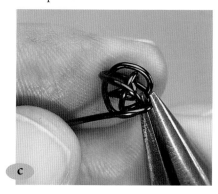

c

Note: If your sphere is too loose and getting hard to hold, pass the tail through the center and gently pull it out from the other side. Continue wrapping. This step can be repeated as needed, although a point may form where you pull the tail from the ball. To prevent this, try to curve the wire as you're pulling it through the ball and, if possible, pull the wire at a gentle curve.

4 Continue wrapping and rotating until the ball is about 1½ inches (3.8 cm) in diameter or your desired size with a tail remaining. Feed the tail through the center of the ball and gently pull it out from the opposite side. Don't pull too hard, or the ball will collapse.

5 Curve the tail flat against the ball and use wire cutters to flush cut the wire to ½ inch (1.3 cm) in length. Use chain-nose pliers to wrap the tail around a wire or two toward the inside of the ball. Make sure the cut end is hidden inside the ball.

hanging the pendant

1 To suspend the ball from a ribbon or other soft cord, thread a piece of scrap wire through its center, use round-nose pliers to turn a small loop at one end (photo d), thread the ribbon through the loop, and use chain-nose pliers to flatten the loop so it will slide between the wires.

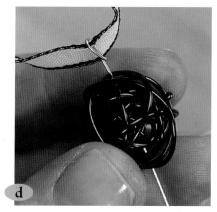

d

Pull the wire back through the ball.

2 Finish the ribbon or cord ends with foldover crimps and add a clasp. Alternatively, you can slide the ball onto a stiff wire neck ring.

Earrings
(with or without beads)

what you will need

- 20-gauge colored craft wire, two 1-foot (30.5 cm) pieces or more for larger balls
- Semiprecious stone, glass, or pearl beads (optional)
- French ear wires
- Basic Tool Kit

making balls without beads

1 Follow the basic instructions for creating a wire ball (see steps 1 through 4 of Forming a Ball) until a 1½-inch (3.8 cm) tail remains. The ball will be approximately ½ inch (1.3 cm) in diameter.

Celestial Orbit Pendant and Earrings

2 Pass the tail though the center of the ball and gently pull it through to the opposite side until the ball is taut but not distorted (photo e). Use chain-nose pliers to bend the tail at a 90° angle on top of the ball (photo f). Use wire cutters to flush cut the wire to loop length and use round-nose pliers to form a simple loop (photo g).

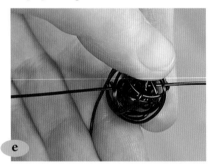
e

f

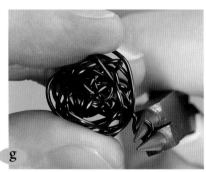
g

3 Repeat steps 1 and 2 with the other piece of wire, visually comparing the ball size to its mate before ending the wrapping.

4 Use flat-nose pliers to open the loop on one ear wire, just as you would open a jump ring. Attach one of the balls to the ear wire loop and close the loop. Repeat this step with the other ball. *Note:* If you want longer earrings, you can also join balls together by using the loop to dangle one ball from a loose wire at the bottom of another ball (photo h).

h

makingballs with beads

1 Start a ball (see page 68). Once you've established a small spherical core, start threading beads onto the wrapping wire. I usually work with only one or two beads at a time so I can space them evenly around the ball (photo i). Continue adding beads to fill "holes" in the sphere and round out the ball visually. You can wrap over some of the beads if you like; this will add visual depth to the ball.

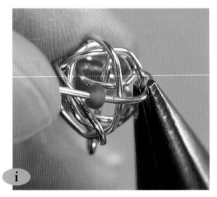
i

2 When the ball is the desired size and at least 1½ inches (3.8 cm) of the wire remains, pass the tail through the center, pulling gently from the opposite side until the wire is taut. Use chain-nose pliers to bend the tail at a 90° angle on top of the ball. Use wire cutters to flush cut the tail to loop length and use round-nose pliers to form a simple loop (see page 18).

3 Repeat steps 1 and 2 to make a matching ball.

4 Attach each ball to an ear wire, as above.

Orbital Necklace

Tiny beads are wrapped into these baubles for a dash of color. If you long for a matching pair of earrings—and who wouldn't?—follow the directions on page 70.

Orbital Necklace

- 22-gauge half-hard sterling silver wire, at least 30 feet (9.1 m)
- 22-gauge half-hard sterling silver wire, two 8-inch (20.3 cm) pieces for clasp, or a commercial hook-and-eye clasp
- Size 11° glass seed beads in several colors
- Basic Tool Kit
- Planishing hammer
- Steel block

getting started

To make this necklace, I selected five different seed beads in a blue/green color palette. I tend to use the same size beads and vary their finishes (shiny, matte, translucent, opaque, and iridescent) to add interest. You don't want the beads to be too light, or their colors will be watered down when they're spaced out around the balls.

I work with 2- to 3-foot (61 to 91.4 cm) lengths of wire for this project; each length yields two or three balls, depending on their size. Small balls—about ¼-inch (6 mm) in diameter—take 10 to 12 inches (25.4 to 30.5 cm) each.

My working design process for this piece is to make two or three balls of each bead color, without thinking much about size. Next, I lay out the balls so they are graduated from small (at the clasp ends) to large toward the center, arranging the bead colors randomly. I then fill in any size or color gaps by making specific balls for specific locations in the necklace. I make some extra-small balls for the very ends of the necklace and extra-large balls for the center, so the size transition is smooth and noticeable, and the necklace reaches 16 to 17 inches (40.6 to 43.2 cm) in length.

making a double-loop ball link

1 Use wire cutters to flush trim the tips of the long wire. Use chain- and round-nose pliers to form a simple loop on one end of the wire (see page 18). Approximately ¼ inch (6 mm) down from the loop, fold the wire loosely back on itself (don't flatten the wire together) to establish a central stem (photo a).

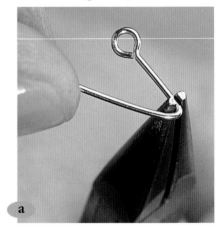

a

Note: The length of the stem determines the size of the ball; ¼ inch (6 mm) is on the small side, so vary the length of the stem for different ball sizes.

2 At the midpoint of the stem, use chain-nose pliers to bend the wrapping wire at a 90° angle. Wrap a loose, open spiral around the stem, working up toward the loop. It works best to hold the pliers parallel to the center post and use your fingers to wrap the wire around them (photo b).

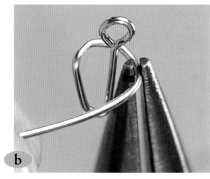

3 Start bending and working the wrapping wire around this central stem to form a sphere, using the instructions provided on page 69. *Note:* The center of this ball is more open than that of the balls on page 69, but as the ball gets bigger, the wrapping wire starts touching the interior wires, creating a more solid and stable ball overall (photo c).

4 When the sphere is roughly blocked out, start threading beads onto the wire and position them around the ball as you wrap (photo d).

5 When the ball is the desired size, pass the wire through its center, starting at the loop end and continuing through to the other side. Pull gently until the wire is taut (photo e).

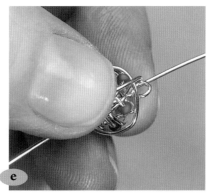

6 Use chain-nose pliers to bend the tail at a 90° angle flat against the ball. Use wire cutters to flush cut the wire to loop length and use round-nose pliers to form a simple loop (photo f). Try to make the loops perpendicular to each other. *Note:* If the starting loop gets slightly buried, grasp it flat with chain-nose pliers and pull it gently so it sticks out slightly.

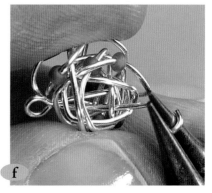

7 Repeat steps 1 through 6 to make an assortment of balls in a variety of colors and sizes—at least 25 for a 17-inch (43.2 cm) necklace.

Orbital Necklace

assembling the necklace

1 Lay out the balls in a graduated necklace pattern, as described on page 72. Link the balls together by connecting the simple loops at the sides of each ball. To connect the loops, first use flat-nose pliers to open a loop on one ball, just as you would a jump ring, then attach the next ball and close the loop.

2 Look for any size or color problems in the necklace. Maybe the ball size gradient is awkward at a point or a color is needed in one area. Make specific balls for these spots until the necklace is the desired length and hangs well.

3 Add a purchased hook-and-eye clasp (due to the size of the balls, a toggle clasp is not recommended). Or try your hand at making a custom hook-and-eye clasp that is incorporated into the balls and blends with the necklace design (see the instructions that follow).

making the eye of the clasp

1 Use round-nose pliers to make a large, double simple loop at one end of one of the 8-inch (20.3 cm) pieces of wire by coiling the wire twice around the base of the pliers. When the wrapping wire meets the cut end of the coil, use chain-nose pliers to bend the wire at a 90° angle that is perpendicular to the loop.

2 Use the wire to make an extra-small ball with beads (see page 70) for one end of your necklace. End the ball in the same way as the others, by pulling the tail through the center of the ball and ending with a double simple loop.

3 If necessary, file the exposed cut end of the double simple loop (see page 13). Connect the ball to the necklace by using flat-nose pliers to open the small loop, just as you would open a jump ring, attaching the ball, and closing the loop.

making the clasp hook

1 Use the second 8-inch (20.3 cm) piece of wire to make a small hook on one end of the wire, as described on page 22. Hammer and finish the hook (see pages 26 to 28).

2 Form an extra-small ball below the hook, measuring the center stem from the point at which the hook's teardrop loop meets the stem.

3 Add the beads while wrapping and end the ball in the same manner as the other balls. Connect the ball to the other necklace end. Adjust the hook opening as necessary to work with the eye.

Bountiful Bubbles Pin

Bubbles of wire cascade over each other, creating a froth of color. Pin this cascade on a coat, jacket, or even a hat.

Bountiful Bubbles Pin

what you will need

- 18-gauge nickel silver wire, approximately 18 inches (45.7 cm)
- 20-gauge colored craft wire, 4 colors in a palette (non-tarnish brass, natural coated copper, burgundy, and red)
- Stick pin end cap
- Basic Tool Kit
- Burnisher
- Pencil or similar object
- Steel block
- Planishing hammer
- Metal file

forming the pin base

1 Use wire cutters to flush trim the tips of the nickel silver wire. Following the directions on page 68, form a ball about ¹/₂-inch diameter (1.2 cm) on one end of the wire. Pull the wrapping wire through the center and trim the stem to 6 inches (15.2 cm)

2 Use a burnisher to make the stem straight (see page 14). About ¹/₄ inch (6 mm) from the ball, form a hook by curving the wire around a pencil or similar object so

the ball points down and slightly out and away from the stem (photo a).

Use a planishing hammer and steel block to hammer the bend. Continue burnishing the bend and the stem until the wire is firm. You have made the pin stem and top, which will provide the base for all the other balls to hang from.

3 Make two 1-loop nickel silver balls that are progressively smaller than the stem ball. Link the first 1-loop ball to the bottom of the stem ball by using flat-nose pliers to open its loop as you would a jump ring, attaching it to one loose wire on the bottom of the stem ball, and closing the loop (photo b). Repeat to add the second 1-loop ball to the bottom of the middle one so the three balls hang in a tapered line.

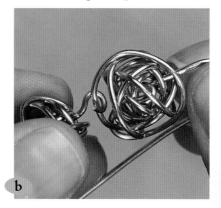

creating the waterfall

1 Make a selection of 1-loop balls, approximately 5 of each color, that have the same size range as the nickel silver balls.

2 Attach the colored balls to the nickel silver balls by linking the loops to loose wires all over the front side of the balls. In general, put the larger balls at the top and the smaller balls at the bottom, but mainly fill in any holes, adding sizes as needed. As you add balls, you may need to reposition attached balls for color distribution and hanging position.

finishing up

1 Use wire cutters to cut the pin stem so it ends a little shorter than where the balls hang. File and finish to a point (see page 13). Cap the stem with a purchased stick pin end cap.

Boutons de Manchette

Parlez-vous Français? If you love French cuffs but lack a basic pair of cufflinks, then create a pair of these elegant adornments to add je ne sais quoi to your own or someone else's special wardrobe.

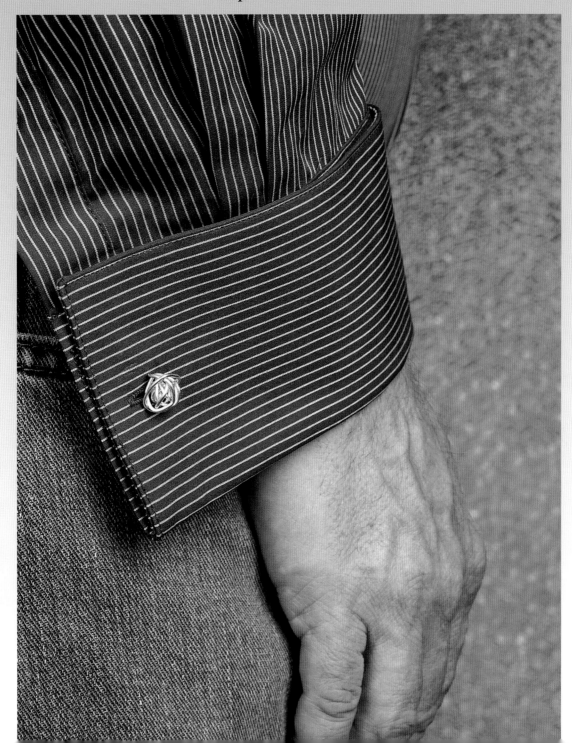

Boutons de Manchette

what you will need

- 18-gauge half-hard sterling silver wire, two 16-inch (40.6 cm) pieces
- 24-gauge half-hard sterling silver wire, two 12-inch (30.5 cm) pieces
- Fine-point permanent marker
- Basic Tool Kit
- Planishing hammer
- Steel block

forming the frames

1 Use wire cutters to flush trim the tips of the pieces of 18-gauge wire. Use your hand to hold the two wires together evenly. Use chain-nose pliers to bend the wires at a 90° angle, 8 inches (20.3 cm) from one end. Measure ¾ inch (1.9 cm) from the bend and mark this point with a fine-tip permanent marker. Use chain-nose pliers to bend the wires at a 90° angle at the mark so the wires make a Z shape with a straight center stem (photo a).

2 Straighten each of the tail pieces by pulling the wire through your thumb and finger.

3 Working with one wire at a time, use a planishing hammer and steel block to gently hammer each bend and the center stem, flipping the wire as you hammer. Don't hammer so hard that the wires flatten—just hard enough to add some structure.

making the center wraps

1 Use your hand to hold one piece of 24-gauge wire perpendicular to the center stem, right at the bend of one of the Z-shaped frames. Leave a tail about 1-inch (2.5 cm) long on the 24-gauge wire. Use the loose wire to make a tight coil (see page 30) around the center stem, working from one bend to the other (photo b). To keep the coil from spinning, use your fingers to hold the starting tail tightly in place (photo c).

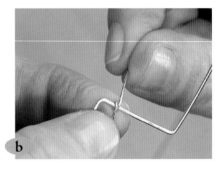

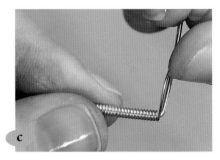

2 When the center stem is completely wrapped, use wire cutters to flush cut both ends and a chain-nose pliers to tuck in the tails.

3 Repeat steps 1 and 2 for the other Z-shaped frame.

adding the ball ends

1 Form one wire end into a ball (see page 68), starting by making a loose circle perpendicular to the hammered bend (photo d). Doing this will create the center around which you'll wrap the sphere. Wrap the wire on all sides of the coiled stem so it stays centered (photo e).

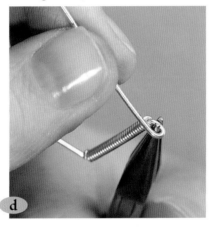

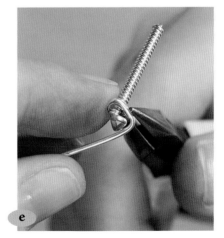

2 When you have about 1¼ inches (3.2 cm) of wire left, use wire cutters to flush cut the wire to ¼ inch (6 mm) in length (photo f). Use chain-nose pliers to fold the wire tightly into the ball, looping it around an interior wire until it's secure.

3 Test this ball to see if it will fit through a cuff buttonhole (thread it one buttonhole at a time). If it's too large, make sure the opposite ball is smaller.

4 Repeat steps 1 through 3 to form balls on all ends.

Breezy Autumn Pendant

*The colors of a bright autumn day accent this airy leaf-shaped pendant.
Glistening white would give it a touch of winter—and a palette of green,
a breath of summer or spring. What is your season?*

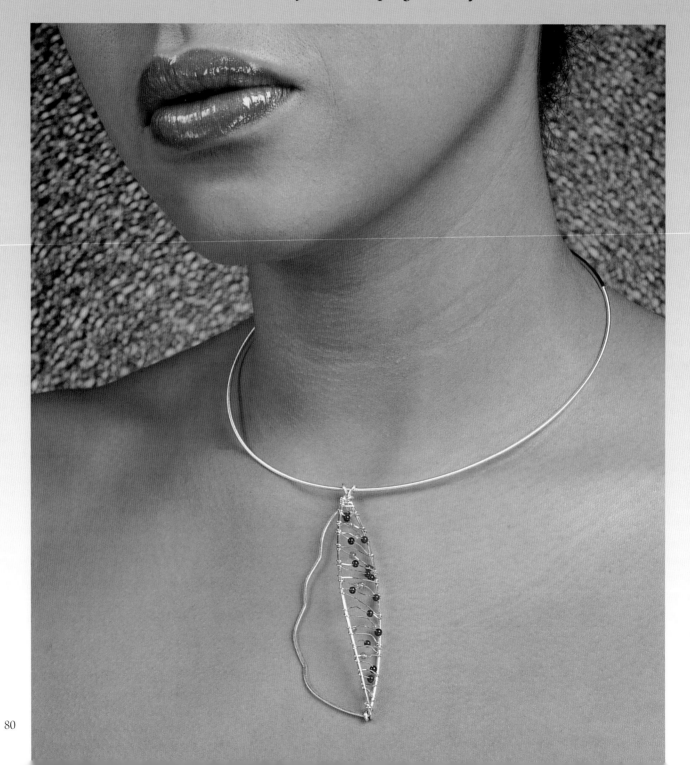

what you will need

- 18-gauge half-hard sterling silver wire, 1 foot (30.5 cm)

- 26-gauge half-hard sterling silver wire, 2 feet (61 cm)

- 2 to 3 mm semiprecious stone, glass, or pearl beads to fit on 26-gauge wire

- 16-inch (40.6 cm) sterling silver neck ring

- Paper

- Pencil

- Basic Tool Kit

- Planishing hammer

- Steel block

getting started

Sketch a leaf shape or gather a favorite from nature to use as inspiration. Don't try to achieve too much detail; just capture a leafy essence.

making the frame

1 Use wire cutters to flush cut the tips of the 18-gauge wire. Use chain-nose pliers to form a soft point in the wire, about 5 inches (12.7 cm) from one end. Working with the natural curve of the wire, bring the two wire ends toward each other in a loose pod/leaf shape. You can also hold the wires together at the top while pushing out the curve from the inside with your thumb (photo a). Make a post by using chain-nose pliers to bend the short end of the wire straight up from the crossing point.

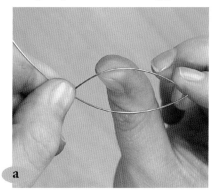

2 While holding the crossing point, pull the long side out so the shape is no longer symmetrical (photo b). To mark the point at which the wire will start wrapping around the post, use chain-nose pliers to form a bend in the long end.

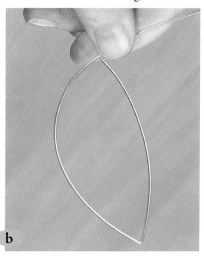

3 Use chain-nose pliers to hold the top of the shape just below the crossing point and wrap the long tail once around the post. The wire should now be pointing toward the front again. Pull this wire down toward the point. Curve it gently over your fingers to give it some dimension. While holding the curved wire in position with one hand, use chain-nose pliers to kink the wire where it meets the point (see page 17).

Breezy Autumn Pendant

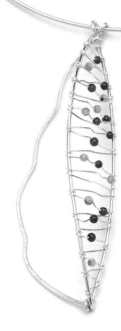

4 Hold the shape firmly while wrapping the wire fully once around the point. You may need to use chain-nose pliers to help pull the wrapping wire tight. End the wrap toward the interior back. Use wire cutters to flush cut the wire, use chain-nose pliers to tuck in the tail, and file and sand the end (see page 13).

5 Reposition and tighten the post's wrap if necessary. Use chain-nose pliers to bend the post at a 90° angle toward the front of the piece. Wrap this tail twice around the thickest part of your round-nose pliers (photo c). End the coil when it meets the top of the pendant. Use wire cutters to flush cut the wire. Position the tail so it's aligned with the coils and doesn't stick out to the side.

6 Pull the two coils slightly apart by grasping each one with flat-nose pliers and bending it slightly away from the center to form a V-shaped, double simple loop that will act as a bail.

7 On the wide, curved side of pendant, add additional bends to the shape as desired to capture the essence of your leaf drawing (photo d). To do this, use chain-nose pliers to form a gentle bend toward the center rib as you hold the frame from the inside and push away from the center rib with your fingers. Adjust shape as you go along (photo e).

8 When the frame shape is complete, use a planishing hammer and steel block to hammer this bent side of the frame, flipping the wire as you hammer, until the shape is flat and firm to the touch. Adjust the frame shape, especially the center rib, if any movement occurred. File and sand any cut ends, and apply any desired finishes to the frame and neck ring.

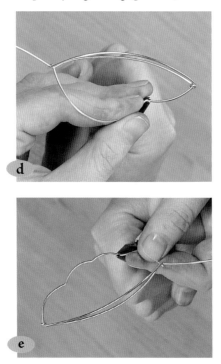

c

d

e

wrapping the form

1 Wrap one end of the 26-gauge wire twice around the outer frame at the bottom, on the smooth, curved unhammered side. Use wire cutters to flush cut the wire and use chain-nose pliers to tuck in the tail.

2 Gently pull the wire over the top of the shape, curving it gently in your fingers, and wrap it over and completely around the center rib (one and one-half rotations) so that it's pointing back toward the outer frame where you started.

3 Pull the wire so it faces the front, and wraps over the top and completely around the outer edge (photo f).

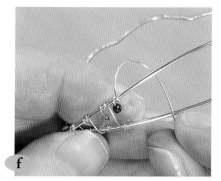

4 Continue wrapping in this manner. Keep the wraps fairly open and thread beads onto the wire occasionally as you go along (photo g). You may add several beads to each wire at the wider parts of the shape. *Note:* Keep the wrapping fairly taut so it supports the center rib, and always hold the center rib as you wrap so it doesn't lean or collapse.

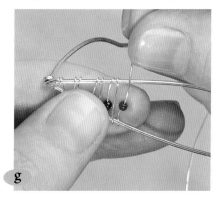

5 End the wrapping with a tight coil on the outer frame edge. Use wire cutters to flush cut the wire and use chain-nose pliers to tuck in the tail.

finishing up

1 To add interest and distribute the beads, use chain-nose pliers to kink the wrapping wires gently (see page 17).

2 Slide the pendant onto the neck ring.

Cosmic Coils Cuff

Orbs and coils of wire wrap around your wrist to create a bold statement in this versatile, unisex bracelet design.

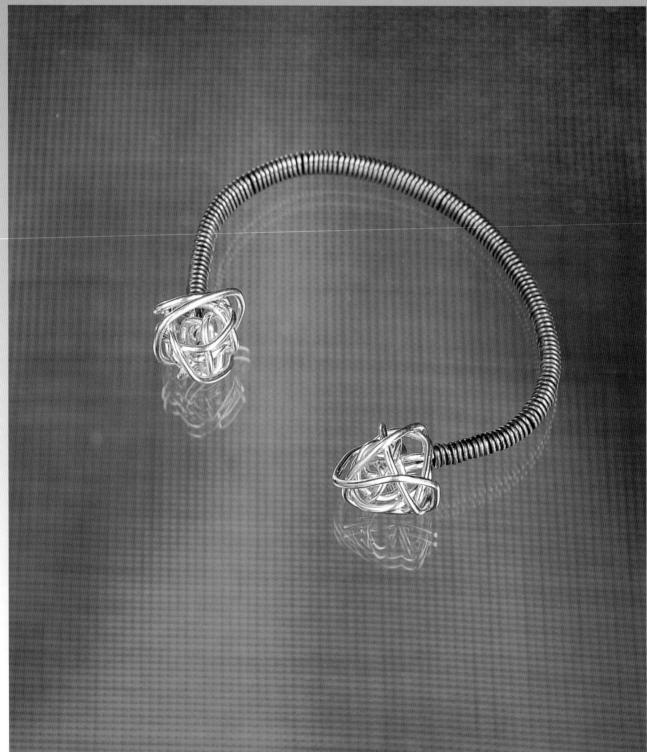

what you will need

- 16-gauge half-hard sterling silver wire, one 31½-inch (80 cm) piece (see Sizing and Preparing Wire below) and one 10-inch (25.4 cm) piece

- 24-gauge copper or other inexpensive binding wire, 18 inches (45.7 cm)

- 20-gauge sterling silver wire, 5½ feet (1.7 m)

- String

- Basic Tool Kit

- Fine-point permanent marker

- Oval bracelet mandrel or large curved object, such as a soup can or baseball bat

- Liver of sulfur

sizing and preparing wire

1 Wrap a piece of string snugly around your wrist. Add approximately 1 inch (2.5 cm) to get the measurement for a comfortably fitted cuff, then add 24 inches (61 cm). Use wire cutters to flush cut a length of 16-gauge wire to this measurement.

2 Use a fine-point permanent marker to mark 1 foot (30.5 cm) from each end of the long piece of 16-gauge wire. Also mark the center of this wire and the center of the 10-inch (25.4 cm) piece of 16-gauge wire. Align the wires at the center marks, then copy the end marks from the long piece to the short piece.

making the cuff frame

1 Use chain-nose pliers to bend the 10-inch (25.4 cm) piece of 16-gauge wire to 90° angles at the marked end points. This piece will align with and wrap around the longer piece of 16-gauge wire. Start making flat, perpendicular coils (see page 20) at these points by wrapping the tails around the tips of your round-nose pliers, but don't make full rotations.

2 Realign the wire with the marks on the long piece of 16-gauge wire, inserting the long wire into the partially-formed coils (photo a). Working with one coil at a time, use your fingers to hold the two 16-gauge wires parallel while using your pliers to fully coil one of the shorter tails (one and one-half rotations is sufficient).

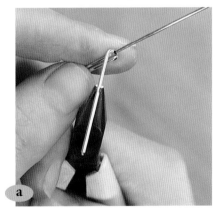

a

Use chain-nose pliers to tighten the coil. Use wire cutters to flush cut the wire and use chain-nose pliers to tighten the tail. Realign the two wires and repeat the process with the other coil.

3 Form a wire ball at one end (see page 68), positioning the coil at the center of the ball.

4 When the first ball is complete, pull the two wires taut and parallel, and form a ball on the other end (photo b).

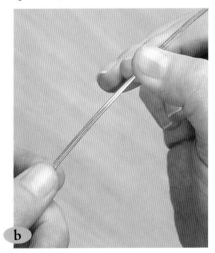

b

Cosmic Coils Cuff

5 If you have a bracelet mandrel, center the bracelet over the wide end and fold the balls toward each other to begin forming a gentle curve. If you don't have a mandrel, fold the bracelet over a soup can or similar object to start forming a wide, smooth curve in the double-wire frame.

You'll do the final forming by hand. Continue to curve the balls gently toward each other, supporting and pushing the wire frame, and working the bracelet into a C shape. Try the bracelet on to determine a comfortable shape and tightness for the form.

wrapping the frame

1 When the shape is finalized, add three or four copper coils to hold the double-wire frame together. Space the coils out on the frame, and make the wraps tight and even.

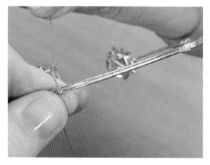

2 Use your hand to hold the 20-gauge wire perpendicular to the double-wire frame, close to one ball, leaving a 2-inch (5.1 cm) tail. Start coiling the wrapping wire tightly around the frame. Wrap carefully and slowly to get started. The coils should be tight and even.

3 After you've made a few wraps, slide the coil close to the ball. Keep wrapping the frame, sliding the coil close to the ball if it moves. When you reach one of the copper sections, either slide the copper coil along if it will move or simply pull one of the ends, and carefully uncoil and discard the wire. **Note:** The curves are the hardest to wrap evenly because there will be small gaps in the wrapping. Just keep the coils as tight and even as possible.

4 When you reach the end, coil as close to the ball as possible. Use wire cutters to flush cut the wire and use chain-nose pliers to tuck in the tail so you won't feel it against your wrist. If necessary, use the starting tail to add coils to fill in any gaps on that end. Then flush cut and tuck the tail.

5 Use chain-nose pliers to flatten any individual coils by grasping the frame and squeezing gently.

6 Oxidize the coiled section by carefully brushing a liver of sulfur solution onto the wires, avoiding the balls as you do (see page 27). Rinse well, dry, and brush the coils with an abrasive scouring pad if desired.

Seed Pod Pendant

Beaded (or not!) this three-dimensional beauty is a
strikingly elegant addition to a simple neck ring.

Seed Pot Pendant

what you will need

- 22-gauge half-hard sterling silver wire, 1 foot (30.5 cm)
- 26-gauge sterling silver wire, 18 inches (45.7 cm)
- 4 to 6 mm semiprecious stone, glass, or pearl beads to fit on 26-gauge wire
- Sterling silver cable neck ring or neck wire
- Basic Tool Kit

making the pod frame

1 Use wire cutters to flush trim the tips of the 22-gauge wire. Use chain-nose pliers to make a sharp bend in the wire, about 3½ inches (8.9 cm) from one end (photo a).

Work with the curve of the wire so the sides curve toward each other (photo b). Cross the wires about 2 inches (5.1 cm) from the point, curving the sides by hand to form a leaflike shape (photo c).

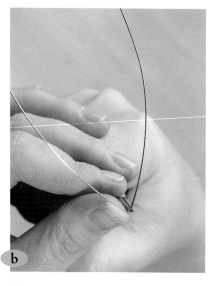

2 To form a stem, use chain-nose pliers to bend the short wire straight up from the crossing point. Hold the wires together with the pliers and wrap the long wire once around the stem by hand so it faces toward the front again (photo d).

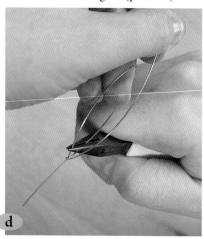

3 Curve this wire down toward the point, supporting it from underneath to add some dimension to the curve (photo e).

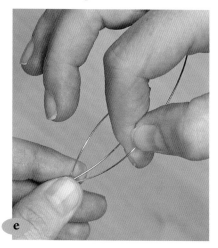

4 Use chain-nose pliers to kink the wire (see page 17) where it meets the point and wrap it fully once around the point. Use wire cutters to flush cut the wire and use chain-nose pliers to tuck the tail to the inside.

5 Use chain-nose pliers to bend the top stem at a 90° angle so it's aligned with the center rib. Use wire cutters to flush cut the wire to loop length and use round-nose pliers to form a simple loop (see page 18).

6 Pull the two side frames toward the back while supporting the center rib. Even out the curves on all ribs and try to make the space between them even, too, so the frame is more dimensional.

wrapping the frame

1 Wrap one end of the 26-gauge wire twice around one rib to secure it. Use chain-nose pliers to tighten the coil. Use wire cutters to flush cut the wire and use chain-nose pliers to tuck the tail to the inside.

2 Wrap the wire over the top of and once around each rib, angling the wire slightly downward with each wrap. When you reach a point at which the place you'll wrap is wide enough, thread a bead onto the wire. Continue wrapping and occasionally adding beads until you reach the point of the frame. Make as many unbeaded wraps as necessary to make this wrapping somewhat similar to the starting wraps.

3 When you're finished wrapping, coil the wire twice around a rib to secure it. Use chain-nose pliers to tighten the coil. Use wire cutters to flush cut the wire and use chain-nose pliers to tuck the tail to the inside.

finishing up

1 Use chain-nose pliers to add kinks to the wrapping wires and position the beads as desired.

2 Slide the pendant onto the cable neck ring, neck wire, or a beaded necklace.

exploring the possibilities

Do you have a penchant for color? Try choosing a simple palette of beads to use on the wraps. If you want a truly custom look (plus a little practice with simple loops shown on page 18), use 24-gauge half-hard or heavier wire to make your own chain by linking beads with simple loops on either end.

Striped Pods Necklace

Everyone will notice these partially-enclosed forms; they'll seem to float around the base of your neck. If you can't stop making these pods, create a much longer strand for a bolder fashion statement.

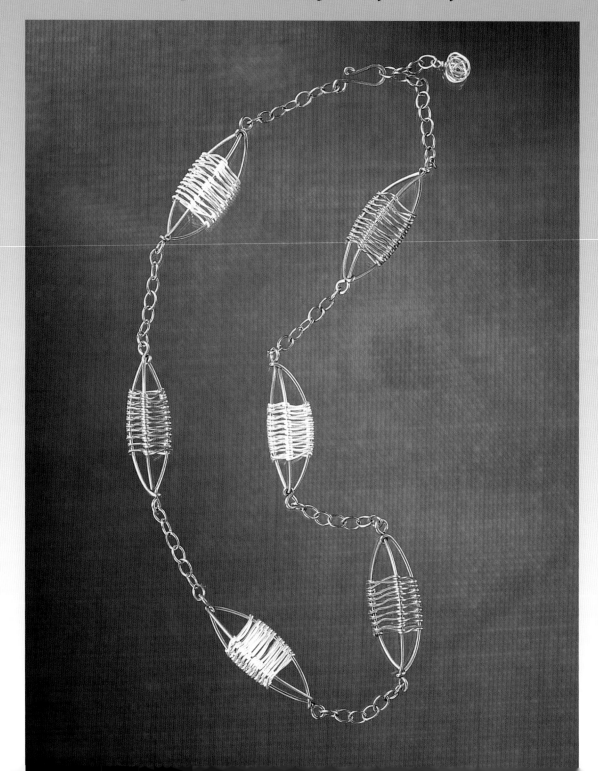

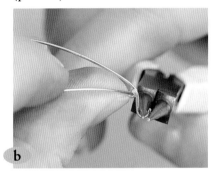

what you will need

- 20-gauge half-hard sterling silver wire, 40 inches (1 m)

- 24-gauge copper wire, 6 feet (1.8 m), plus an additional 8-inch (20.3 cm) piece*

- 24-gauge sterling silver wire, 6 feet (1.8 m)

- Sterling silver chain, 1 foot (30.5 cm)

- Sterling silver clasp, commercial or handmade

- Basic Tool Kit

- Liver of sulfur

*Use coated copper craft wire if you don't want it to discolor.

making the pod links

1 Use wire cutters to flush cut the 20-inch (50.8 cm) piece of 20-gauge wire. Use chain-nose pliers to make a sharp bend in the wire, 2¼ inches (5.7 cm) from the flush-cut end.

2 Make a three-sided pod (see page 88), but make this pod's overall length about 1¼ inches (3.2 cm). After you wrap the center rib around the point, position the wire so it sticks straight out the back, perpendicular to the point (photo a).

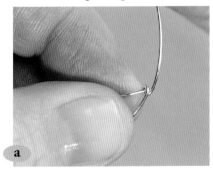

Use wire cutters to flush cut the wire to loop length and use round-nose pliers to form a simple loop (photo b).

3 As you would if you were making a three-sided pod, bend the top stem and form a simple loop, making it perpendicular to the first loop. Gently curve the side ribs toward the back, and then adjust the curve on all the ribs and even out their spacing.

4 Repeat steps 1 through 3 to make six pod-link frames

Striped Pods Necklace

assembling the necklace

1 Oxidize the frames, chain, and clasp if desired (see page 27).

2 Use wire cutters to flush cut a 24-inch (61 cm) piece of 24-gauge copper or silver wire. Anchor and wrap the wire around the center of one pod, starting and ending the wraps ¼ to ½ inch (.6 to 1.3 cm) from each end. Repeat for each pod, wrapping three with silver and three with copper wire.

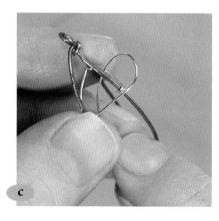

c

3 Use wire cutters to cut the chain into six 1¼-inch (3.2 cm) lengths and one 2-inch (5.1 cm) length.

4 Use flat-nose pliers to open one of the loops on a pod, just as you would open a jump ring, and link it to the end of one of the short pieces of chain. Close the loop. Continue linking the pods and chain together, alternating copper and silver pod links. Finish by connecting the long chain.

5 Use wire cutters to flush cut the 8-inch (20.3 cm) length of 24-gauge copper wire and follow the instructions on page 68 to make a tiny wire ball, leaving a tail at least 3 inches (7.6 cm) long. Form a wrapped loop with the tail (see page 19), inserting the loop through the last open link of the long chain before you make the wrap. This is your extender chain.

6 Attach a simple handmade hook-and-eye clasp (see page 22)—or a purchased clasp that will fit your chain links—to the other end of the chain.

exploring the possibilities

Do you love the airiness of the Seedpod Pendant on page 87? Try wrapping these smaller pod links using that same technique. Use 2 to 3mm beads and a delicate chain for a lightweight and airy necklace that floats on your collarbone.

Suspended Pod Stickpin

Be prepared! Admirers of this four-sided, golden pod stickpin may be tempted to pluck it right off of your lapel.

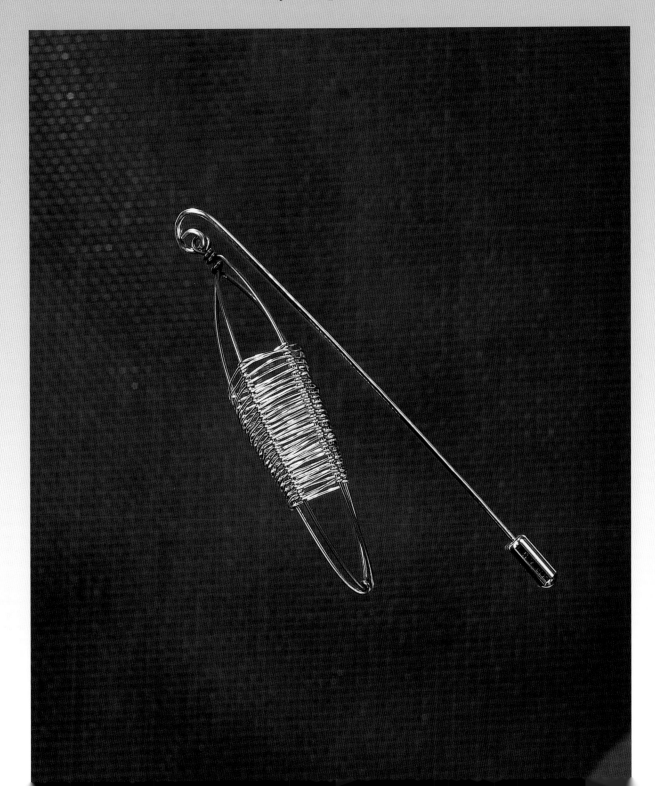

Suspended Pod Stickpin

what you will need

- 18-gauge half-hard gold-filled wire, 5 inches (12.7 cm)
- 20-gauge half-hard sterling silver wire, 18 inches (45.7 cm)
- 26-gauge half-hard gold-filled wire, 6 feet (1.8 m)
- Brass or gold-plated stickpin end cap
- Basic Tool Kit
- Planishing hammer
- Steel block
- Burnisher
- Liver of sulfur (optional)

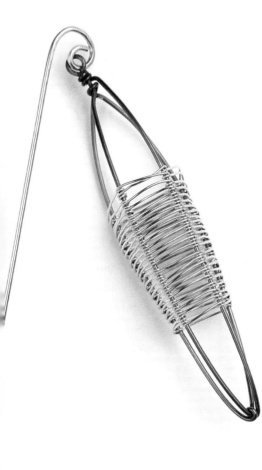

making the pin stem

1 Use wire cutters to flush trim the tips of the 18-gauge wire. Form a large loop at one end by wrapping the wire around the large part of round-nose pliers and continue wrapping as if you were beginning a large open spiral. This forms the curled shepherd's-hook shape from which the dangle will hang.

2 Straighten and harden the pin stem (see pages 14 and 15). Use the planishing hammer and steel block to hammer the hook and spiral lightly until the shape is firm.

making the pod frame

1 Use chain-nose pliers to form a sharp bend in the 20-gauge wire, about 4 inches (10.2 cm) from one end, working with the curve of the wire. Curve the wires toward each other, forming them into a pod shape by pushing from the inside of the form. Cross the wires about 2½ inches (6.4 cm) from the point.

2 At the crossing point, use chain-nose pliers to bend the short wire straight up to form a stem. Hold the crossed wires in the pliers and wrap the long wire once around this stem (photo a).

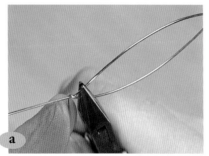

3 When the long wire is at the front, curve it down toward the point, supporting the curve on the inside to give the form dimension. Use chain-nose pliers to kink the wire (photo b) where it meets the point and then wrap the wire once around the point until it's pointing toward the back side again (photo c).

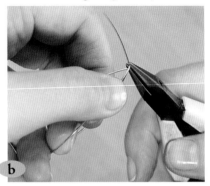

4 Use chain-nose pliers to adjust and tighten the point wrap. Pull the long wire up toward the stem; try to make the curve symmetrical (photo d).

d

5 Now form the fourth rib. Use chain-nose pliers to kink the wire where it meets the stem, just above the first wrap, and then continue coiling twice around the stem. **Note:** To get a tight coil, use the pliers to hold both the top of the fourth rib (where you currently grasp) and an additional rib as you coil the wire with your other hand. This will help keep the fourth rib from wrapping tighter as the coil is formed around the stem (photo e). Use wire cutters to flush cut the wire and use chain-nose pliers to tuck in the tail. Make any necessary adjustments to the

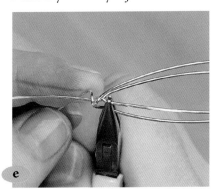

e

form: squeeze coils so they stack tightly, smooth any kinks in the ribs, and perfect the point tip.

6 If desired, oxidize or apply any finishes to the frame (see pages 27 and 28).

wrapping the pod

1 Use wire cutters to cut a 3-foot (91.4 cm) length of 26-gauge wire. Attach one end of the wire by coiling it twice around one rib, about ¾ inch (1.9 cm) down from the top. Tighten the coil while holding the rib and the long wire in place. Use wire cutters to flush cut the tail and use chain-nose pliers to tuck it to the inside.

2 Pull the wire across to the next rib, use chain-nose pliers to kink it, and then hold the rib and the long wire in place as you wrap around the rib once. Repeat until you're ready to wrap the rib where you first started. On this first rotation around the pod, be sure not to pull the wrapping wire so tightly that you distort the shape or pull the ribs out of placement.

3 At this point, wrap the wire above the starting coil, then pull the wire back in line to make your next wraps below each previous wrap.

4 Continue wrapping evenly until you are left with about 2 inches (5.1 cm) of wrapping wire.

Note: If the side wraps aren't level, coiling twice around a rib should help you align them. Repeat as needed.

5 End the wrapping wire by coiling it tightly twice around a rib. Use wire cutters to flush cut the wire and use chain-nose pliers to tuck the tail to the inside. Attach another 3-foot (91.4 cm) length of wrapping wire by starting on the opposite rib to offset any gaps.

6 Continue wrapping to about ¾ inch (1.9 cm) from the bottom, or until the wrapped section is centered on the pod. To end the wrapping wire, coil twice around a rib above the last coil on that rib. Use wire cutters to flush cut the wire and use chain-nose pliers to tuck in the tail.

7 Adjust the wrapping wires as desired to straighten them and correct their spacing. ***Tip:*** Use your fingers and thumbnails; pliers are too large to fit between the tight wraps.

finishing up

1 Form a simple loop with the pod frame stem, positioning it the way you want it to hang from the pin stem (see page 18).

2 Use wire cutters to flush cut the pin stem to 3½ inches (8.9 cm) or to your desired length. File the end to a point and finish it as shown on page 13.

3 Use flat-nose pliers to open the pod's loop, just as you would open a jump ring. Hang the pod from the spiral hook and close the loop. Cap the pointed end of the pin with the end cap.

Captured Memories Pendant

A singular pebble or shell handpicked on a summer beach stroll or winter hike by the creek can be showcased in this pendant and cherished year round.

what you will need

- 22-gauge half-hard sterling silver wire, 10 inches (25.4 cm)
- 26-gauge sterling silver wire, 4 feet (1.2 m)
- Small object, approximately ½ inch (1.3 cm)
- Small (2 mm) semiprecious stone, pearl, or glass beads that coordinate with the object and can fit on the 26-gauge wire
- ½ inch (1.3 cm)-wide ribbon, 18 inches (45.7 cm)
- 2 sterling silver foldover ribbon crimps
- Sterling silver clasp and jump rings
- Basic Tool Kit

getting started

You can make your frame with 22- or 20-gauge half-hard wire, and the wraps can be with 24- or 26-gauge wire.

Use any object that can't slip between the wires; you may need to adjust the wire measurements if your object is much larger or smaller than described here (see the last section in these instructions).

When I make these forms, I eyeball all measurements because I like the slightly uneven look, and it's hard to measure, mark, and adjust for wire thicknesses as you're wrapping.

To oxidize your box, oxidize the frame and the 26-gauge wire before you start the wrapping.

making the box frame

1 Lay the object down on the work surface. As you form the initial square frame outline (in step 2), lay it around your object to make sure the height and width will hold your object. You can build in as much or as little space as you want for your object to move around, but due to the nature of the wrapping, the bottom crossbars and the top arms need to be similar lengths to each other (i.e., you can't make a wide flat rectangle).

2 Use wire cutters to flush trim the tips of the 22-gauge wire. Use chain-nose pliers to form a 90°angle about 3½ inches (8.9 cm) from one end. Bend another 90° angle about ⅝ inch (1.5 cm) away from the first bend so the sides are parallel (photo a). Straighten the sides with your fingers. In general, keep pulling the wire straight with each bend.

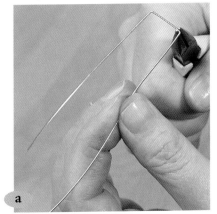

3 About 1 inch (2.5 cm) up each side, use chain-nose pliers to bend the wires towards each other at 90° angles to block out a rectangle (photo b). Your object needs to fit within this outline, so adjust measurements if needed. Bend the short tail straight up at a 90° angle from the center of the top edge to form a stem (photo c). The distance from the top rectangle corner to this stem is what we refer to as the top arm length; there will be four of these.

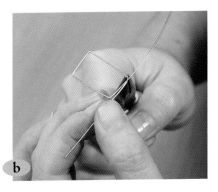

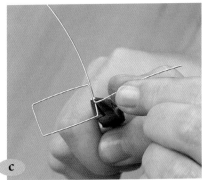

Captured Memories Pendant

4 Use chain-nose pliers to hold the long wire where it crosses the stem, creating the second arm (photo d). Form a 90° angle that sits perpendicular to the stem.

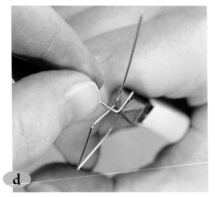

d

Holding the chain-nose pliers at the top arm-length distance, bend another 90° angle in the long wire so it points straight down to form the third side (photo e). Try to make this top edge arm about same length as the two others.

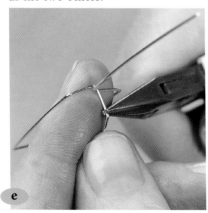

e

5 Use chain-nose pliers to bend the long wire at a 90° angle so it crosses under the rectangle frame (photo f). Try to get these bottom wires to touch if possible.

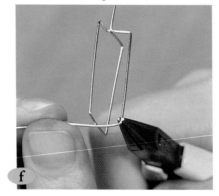

f

6 Use chain-nose pliers to bend the wire at a 90° angle so it's pointing up towards the top again (photo g). Try to make the bottom cross bars the same length.

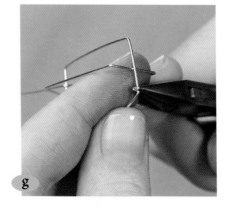

g

Straighten the side and bend the wire at a 90° angle towards the stem to form the fourth top arm. Form the bend so the wire hits the stem above the first wire you bent around the stem (the third arm) in Step 3.

7 Use chain-nose pliers to firmly hold the wire in position at the point where it meets the stem. Coil the long end snugly around the stem, using chain-nose pliers to tighten the coil after the first wrap, and then coiling twice more. Use wire cutters to flush cut the wire and use chain-nose pliers to tuck in the tail (photo h).

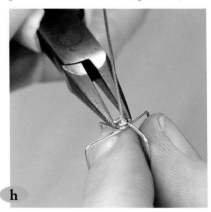

h

wrapping the box

1 Use wire cutters to flush cut 24 inches (61 cm) of 26-gauge wire. Starting at the bottom of the box, leave a short tail and wrap the wire diagonally at the crossing point of the two cross bars to secure them together (photo i).

Use wire cutters to flush cut the tail and use chain-nose pliers to tuck it to the inside.

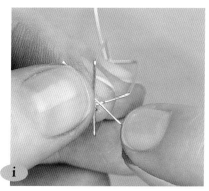

2 Establish the bottom center of the box by wrapping the wire over and once around each rib (photo j). Support and hold the frame by putting a finger inside if possible; try not to squeeze the ribs from the outside or the frame will distort. Hold the point where the wrapping wire crosses the rib and pull the wrapping wire tightly around each rib, lining up the wraps closely.

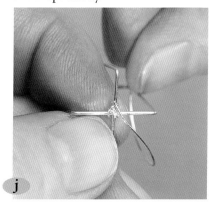

3 As the center grows to about the midpoint of the bottom crossbars, start to open up the wrapping and occasionally thread a bead onto the wire between wraps. Still pull the wrapping wire tight, but space the wraps away from each other by holding the wire as you wrap around the rib. **Note:** Keep sliding the crossbars so they are centered. If one bar becomes a lot longer, make a double coil around that rib to keep the wrapping fairly even to the corners.

4 Wrap the bottom until each corner is covered. Leave the wrapping wire dangling.

5 Coil the end of the remaining 26-gauge wire tightly around one of the top arms. Choose a long arm and one that is in a low position compared to the others. Be sure to coil the wire so that the working end will be wrapping in the opposite direction as the bottom wrapping wire when looking down from the top (photo k).

Use wire cutters to flush cut the tail and use chain-nose pliers to tuck it to the inside.

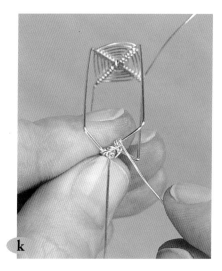

Captured Memories Pendant

6 Wrap the top in the same way as the bottom, starting tight and then opening up (photo l). Wrap in an open manner and occasionally thread beads onto the wrapping wire to the corners and then down the sides one or two times around the form.

7 Your object should still fit easily through the openings, so now wrap one or two times around the box with the bottom wrapping wire, adding beads as desired, making sure your object can still fit inside (photo m).

8 When there's just enough room to fit your object, pop it inside the box. Be sure to block the large unwrapped openings with your fingers so the object doesn't fall out. Continue wrapping with the bottom wire to the midpoint, and then wrap with the top wire to the midpoint, threading beads onto the wire for some of the wraps.

9 End the wrapping wires by coiling them tightly around a rib. Use wire cutters to flush cut the tails and use chain-nose pliers to tuck them to the inside.

finishing up

1 Adjust the spacing of the wrapping wires and use chain-nose pliers to add kinks as desired (see page 17). Choose the side that you want to face front and bend the top stem at a 90° angle facing that side. Use wire cutters to flush cut the stem wire to loop length and use round-nose pliers to form a simple loop (see page 18).

2 Pass the ribbon through the loop and trim to desired length. Finish the ribbon ends with foldover crimps. Add a clasp with jump rings.

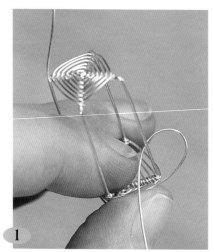

l

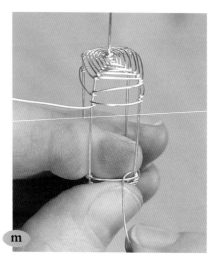

m

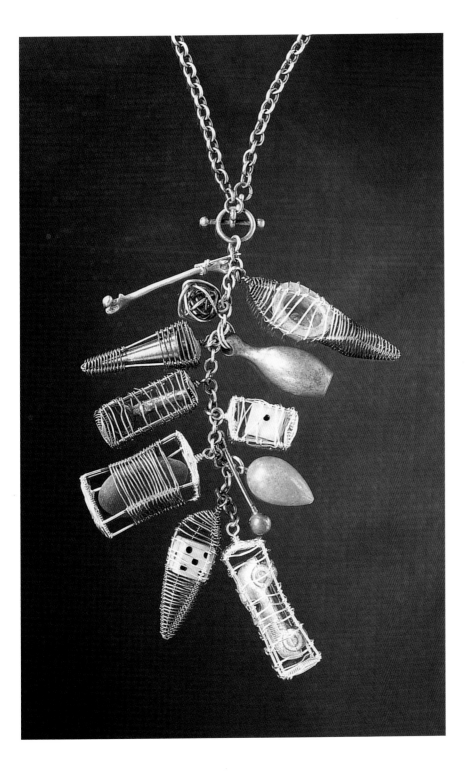

You can try different straps other than ribbon to change the style of this necklace. If you like the look of chain but want to keep the delicate open wrap look of the cube, try using multiple strands of a delicate chain. The variation shown uses three strands and joins the chain to the clasp with wrapped loops and beads that coordinate with the captured object.

Ready to really experiment? Try making different types of shapes and found objects. You can try 4-sided pods like the stickpin (page 94) or pyramids (page 102). You can wrap them in different ways to hide or reveal different object parts and play with oxidation techniques.

Inverted Pyramid Pendant

Need a bit of drama? This exaggerated, inverted pyramid pendant
makes even a casual outfit one that's sure to be remembered.

what you will need

- 20-gauge half-hard sterling silver wire, 16 inches (40.6 cm)
- 24-gauge sterling silver wire, 16 feet (4.9 m)
- Sterling silver headpin (commercial or handmade)
- Rubber cord, 30 inches (76.2 cm)
- 4 to 6 mm decorative bead
- Basic Tool Kit
- Liver of sulfur (optional)

making the frame

1 Use wire cutters to flush trim the tips of the 20-gauge wire. Use chain-nose pliers to make a sharp bend about 3½ inches (8.9 cm) from one end of the 20-gauge wire. This establishes the bottom point of the pyramid, so adjust the point and the wires to the angles you want. Straighten the wires with your fingers.

2 Use chain-nose pliers to bend each side of the wire about 2¼ inches (5.7 cm) from the point so they are positioned at sharp angles to each other (photo a).

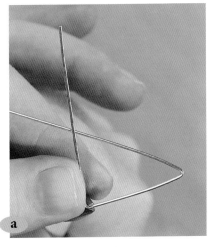

To form a stem, use the pliers to bend the short tail at a 90° angle straight up from the midpoint (photo b). The distance from the top triangle corner to this stem is the arm length. There will be four top arms.

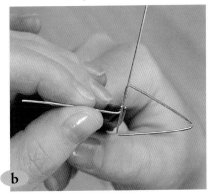

3 Use chain-nose pliers to hold the point where the long wire meets the stem and make a 90° bend around the stem (photo c).

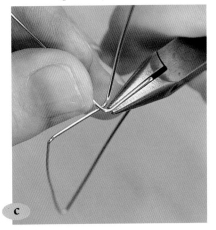

4 Use chain-nose pliers to grasp the long wire on the other side of the stem so when you bend the wire, you'll have another top arm the same length as the first one. Make a sharp bend in the long wire to direct it down toward the point. Straighten this side with your fingers and get the wire to angle toward the point.

Inverted Pyramid Pendant

5 Use chain-nose pliers to bend a 90° angle in the long wire so it lies across and touches the outside bottom of the point (photo d).

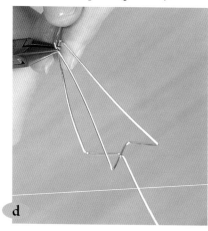

d

Use round-nose pliers to hold the bend and form a simple loop by wrapping the wire around the outside jaw of the pliers (photo e).

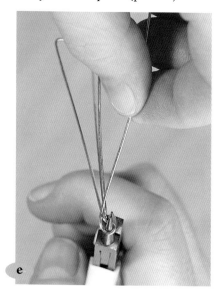

e

6 Use chain-nose pliers to hold the loop while you work on positioning and straightening the long wire to establish the fourth rib.

7 Use chain-nose pliers to bend the top side at a sharp angle toward the stem so the fourth top arm hits above the other wire that you bent around the stem in step 3 (photo f).

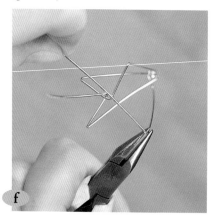

f

Use chain-nose pliers to hold this arm in place and coil the long wire snugly around the stem. Use the pliers to tighten the coil after the first wrap, and then coil the wire twice more. Use wire cutters to flush cut the wire and use chain-nose pliers to tuck in the tail.

8 Adjust the point loop and the overall frame shape as desired.

wrapping the pyramid

1 Use wire cutters to flush cut 3 feet (91.4 cm) of 24-gauge wire. Coil one end of the wire around one of the ribs at the pyramids point (choose a rib that's not part of the loop). Use wire cutters to flush cut the tail and use chain-nose pliers to tuck it to the inside.

2 Align and hold the point while wrapping the wire tightly once around the base of the loop (photo g). Start wrapping over and around each rib. Do your best to make the wrapping as tight as possible.

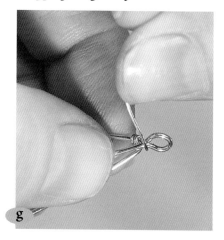

g

3 Wrap all around the form three or four times and then leave the wrapping wire hanging.

4 Use wire cutters to flush cut 4 feet (1.2 m) of 24-gauge wire. Coil one end of this second wrapping wire around one of the form's top arms (choose an arm that's long and positioned lower than the others). Set up the wire so that when you look down on the form, it will wrap in the opposite direction to the bottom wire.

5 Use the new wire to start wrapping over and around each arm. As you wrap toward the corners, if any arm is longer and the wrapping isn't even with the other sides, simply wrap around the rib twice so you reach the corners at about the same time.

6 Wrap over the corners and start down the shape. When you're near the end of the wrapping wire, coil it tightly around one rib. Use wire cutters to flush cut the wire and use chain-nose pliers to tuck the tail to the inside.

7 Continue wrapping with the bottom wire until about 1 inch (2.5 cm) remains. When you need to add another piece of wire, start the new wire on a rib that's diagonal to the place at which you ended a piece. Since this form is tightly wrapped, try not to end your last piece of wire on top of another wire end, as this will create a large gap in the wrapping.

8 When the piece is totally wrapped, use your fingers to adjust the wire spacing to even it out.

finishing up

1 Use chain-nose pliers to bend the stem at a 90° angle. Use wire cutters to flush cut the wire to loop length and use round-nose pliers to form a large, simple loop, sized for your cord (see page 19).

2 If desired, finish the pyramid by oxidizing it with liver of sulfur. If you are oxidizing, also oxidize about 8 inches (20.3 cm) of 24-gauge wire for your cord finishing and the appropriate-gauge wire or headpin for your bead dangle.

3 Slip a bead onto a headpin and then attach it to the bottom loop of the pyramid with a wrapped loop (see page 37).

4 Slide the pendant onto the rubber cord. Overlap the ends of the cord by 1½ inches (3.8 cm) or enough to reach your desired length, but leave the cord long enough to slide over your head.

Inverted Pyramid Pendant

5 Holding the cords parallel and tightly, position the remaining 24-gauge wire ¼ inch (6 mm) from one cord end so it sits perpendicular to the cord. Leave a ½-inch (1.3 cm) tail sticking out to one side. Hold the tail wire against the cords and pull the wrapping end once around firmly, but don't tighten it so much that it cuts into the rubber. Make three or four more wraps to reach the center (photo h).

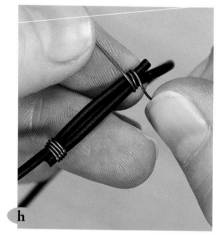

h

Use wire cutters to flush cut the wire and use chain-nose pliers to tuck the tail between the two cords and partially under the coil (photo i). Trim and tuck the starting tail in the same way.

i

6 Repeat step 5 to finish the other cut end of the cord. Trim any excess rubber.

7 Position the pendant in the center of the cord. Hold the side cords together and create a wrapped section ½ inch (1.3 cm) up from the pendant, following the same process as described above.

Gallery

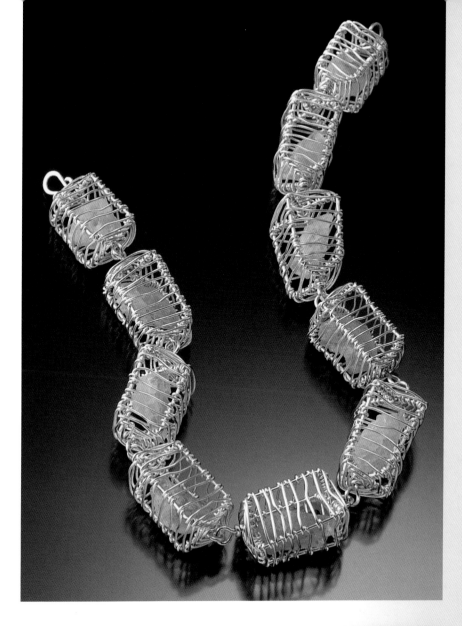

top left: **Kathy Frey,** *Half Wrap Pod Earrings,* 1999
Oxidized sterling silver, pearls
Photo by Larry Sanders

top right: **Kathy Frey,** *Caged Aquamarine Bracelet,* 2006
Sterling silver, rough-cut aquamarines
Photo by Larry Sanders

bottom right: **Kathy Frey,** *Pod Rings (aka Finger Sprouts),* 2006
Sterling silver, oxidized sterling silver, carnelian, Mexican fire opal
Photo by Larry Sanders

top left: **Kathy Frey**, *Black Gold Pyramids*, 2005
sterling silver, 14K gold
Photo by Larry Sanders

top right: **Kathy Frey**, *Anemone Brooch*, 2005
Sterling silver
Photo by Larry Sanders

bottom right: **Kathy Frey**, *Riverstone Bangles*, 2002
Sterling silver, oxidized sterling silver
Photo by Larry Sanders

opposite page: **Kathy Frey**, *Graduated Pearl Boxes*, 2006
Oxidized sterling silver, pearls
Photo by Larry Sanders

top: **Kathy Frey,**
9 Leaves Necklace, 1999
Sterling silver
Photo by Larry Sanders

bottom left: **Kathy Frey, *Wraped Band Stone Rings***, 2006
Sterling, chalcedony, ocean jasper
Photo by Larry Sanders

bottom right: **Kathy Frey,**
Pyramid Bundle Ring, 2006
Oxidized sterling silver, 14K gold
Photo by Larry Sanders

Acknowledgments

Many people have supported me during the process of developing this book, but the people I really need to thank are those at Lark. Nicole McConville needs to be credited with having the vision for this project and the patience to answer all my questions. This book never would have come to fruition without the creative efforts, technical ability, and enthusiasm of Terry Taylor, Jean Campbell, and Kathy Holmes who helped develop and shape my ideas into a finished and understandable format.

Over the years other jewelers, friends, and metal-smiths have helped me to hone my skills. Thanks to Pam Robinson at Lillstreet in Chicago for technical instruction, and to my jeweler friends Janice Ho, Alley Maranto, and Melissa Borrell for creative energy and ideas.

Writing this book wouldn't have been possible without the assistance of Vanessa Walilko and Holly Wherry who kept my studio running smoothly.

I thank my husband, Dan, for his support and understanding for all the time put into this project and my jewelry career as a whole. All my family and friends have been wonderful during the process, and I appreciate the enthusiastic anticipation they've all shared with me... and now I can say the book is finally here!

Index